SOCRATES THE ROWER

How Rowing Informs Philosophy

John Frohnmayer

SOCRATES THE ROWER

How Rowing Informs Philosophy

John Frohnmayer

COMMON GROUND PUBLISHING 2016

First published in 2016
as part of the New Directions in the Humanities Book Imprint

Common Ground Publishing
2001 South First Street, Suite 202
University of Illinois Research Park
Champaign, IL
61820

Copyright © John Frohnmayer 2016

All rights reserved. Apart from fair dealing for the purposes of study, research, criticism, or review as permitted under the applicable copyright legislation, no part of this book may be reproduced by any process without written permission from the publisher.

Library of Congress Cataloging-in-Publication Data

Names: Frohnmayer, John (John E.), author.
Title: Socrates the rower : how rowing informs philosophy / John Frohnmayer.
Description: Champaign, IL : Common Ground Publishing, 2016. | Includes bibliographical references and index.
Identifiers: LCCN 2016030031 (print) | LCCN 2016041822 (ebook) | ISBN 9781612299150 (hbk : alk. paper) | ISBN 9781612299167 (pbk : alk. paper) | ISBN 9781612299174 (pdf)
Subjects: LCSH: Rowing--Philosophy.
Classification: LCC GV791 .F76 2015 (print) | LCC GV791 (ebook) | DDC 797.12/301--dc23
LC record available at https://lccn.loc.gov/2016030031

Front Cover Photo Credit: Row2k, used with permission
Back Cover Photo Credit: Tony Hayden, Aloha Photographic Studio

Table of Contents

Introduction — *xi*

Chapter 1
The Perfect Catch — 1

Chapter 2
Why Philosophy? — 9

Chapter 3
Why Row? — 14

Chapter 4
Plato (circa 428–348 BCE) — 18

Chapter 5
Tools of the Trade — 21

Chapter 6
A Commercial for Philosophy — 26

Chapter 7
Aristotle (384–327 BCE) — 30

Chapter 8
The Stroke — 32

Chapter 9
Courage — 36

Chapter 10
Augustine (354–430 CE): The Rake, the Saint, and the Genius   39

Chapter 11
Anatomy of a Race   43

Chapter 12
Desiderius Erasmus (1466–1536)   48

Chapter 13
Rowing as Healing   50

Chapter 14
Descartes (1596–1650)   54

Chapter 15
The Workout   57

Chapter 16
Jeremy Bentham (1748–1832) and
John Stuart Mill (1806–1873)   60

Chapter 17
Gear   65

Chapter 18
Immanuel Kant (1724–1804) and
William Blake (1757–1827)   68

Chapter 19
Drowning, Hypothermia, and Other Unpleasantries   72

Chapter 20
Friedrich Nietzsche (1844–1900)   76

Chapter 21
Coaches and Coxswains	81

Chapter 22
Kierkegaard (1813–1855)	86

Chapter 23
Famous Crabs	88

Chapter24
Sartre (1905–1980)	92

Chapter 25
Stamina and the Stoics	94

Chapter 26
Ludwig Wittgenstein (1889–1951)	100

Chapter 27
Religion	104

Chapter 28
Opening Day	107

Chapter 29
Martin Luther King, Jr. (1929–1968)
and Michael Walzer (1935–)	110

Chapter 30
Chauvinistic, Sexist, Misanthropic Bastards	113

Chapter 31
Jurisprudence	116

Chapter 32
Sex, Rowing, and Philosophy   119

Chapter 33
Choking   122

Chapter 34
Viktor Frankl (1905–1997)   125

Chapter 35
Time   128

Chapter 36
Jefferson, James, Dewey, and Rorty   131

Chapter 37
Rowology Redux   137

Chapter 38
The Long Haul   142

Appendices   145

Introduction

This is a book about rowing and philosophy, jumbled together in the blender we call life. Rowing might seem like an unlikely avenue leading to the secrets of a life well lived, but many of life's flashes of clarity arrive unbidden, and this book is an explanation of how they snuck up on me. While our bodies are busy getting sweaty and our lungs are crying for mercy, our minds are often on a frolic and detour that leads to some cleansing insights.

I think both rowing and philosophy are fun. Both nourish the body and the mind. Both lead to heath. Both renew our spirit. One is often a metaphor for the other. But most importantly, understanding rowing is a portal, an entryway, to understanding philosophy and vice versa. My academic philosopher friends might retort: "Balderdash," and my rowing buddies might loudly and profanely utter a barnyard phrase, but it is true. Philosophy and rowing have a lot to say to each other.

Just as the rowing shell skims the surface of the water, this book skims the surface of philosophy, recounting its significant figures with astonishing superficiality. There are no footnotes; no citations to sources; no in depth analysis. It is meant to be an introduction, a fishhook in the cheek, a glimpse of what could be really worthwhile immersing oneself in for a lifetime. As such it might be used by teachers, introductory students, athletes in any sport, and those of us who are struggling to understand what the hell is going on in our lives.

Both philosophy and rowing are kinetic, so whether you pick this book up and read it, or toss it forcefully into the corner, you prove my point.

Chapter 1

The Perfect Catch

> "All are lunatics, but he who can analyze his delusion is called a philosopher." Ambrose Bierce d.1914

Growing up, my father's idea of a joke was to tell us something absurdly untrue, like he was the coxswain on the University of Washington crew. He didn't go there, didn't cox and didn't know sicum about rowing. But that recurring joke/falsehood/family yuk implanted rowing in my subconscious so that one morning thirty some years later when I saw crew boats on the Willamette in Portland, I thought that this is something I should try.

So I took a class at Station L Rowing Club. I have always loved that name—it reeks of a kind of dusty, military, historical club with eons of sweat and tradition. In reality it is named after the Pacific Power substation whose dock the club used. The club's equipment consisted of a couple of very old, very heavy Pocock cedar eights housed in an old wooden chip barge with a blue metal pole building on it. The barge was tired and rotten and desperately wanted to sink so periodically we would arrive and find the sump pump had quit and the decks were awash.

The Museum of Science and Industry acquired the premises and we were replaced with a submarine that didn't have any interest in going under. I spent a good part of a sabbatical from my law firm trying to find another moorage but downtown Portland waterfront property was at a premium, the chip barge ugly and the club without funds.

Finally, a friend who had just constructed an office building, said we could moor there. I was so thrilled that I didn't seek permission from any official, a friendly tug company gave us a shove down river, we lassoed a couple of pilings and were back in business underneath the "hard to hit" Fremont Bridge.

The move went so smoothly, after all of our apprehension that the barge, once unleashed, would rampage down the Columbia and out to sea, that we wanted perfect and the ramp was slightly offset. Alan Stewart and I thought, "no problem" so we unbolted it and the two ton ramp fell into the water. I am not sure how Alan got it back up. I decided at that point that lawyers shouldn't be turning wrenches.

And that is where Station L stayed as long as I was affiliated. The location wasn't great, the barge still longed to sink and an occasional concrete missile would fly off the bridge, through our roof and a couple of boats, but we kept on keeping on.

When I left to be Chairman of the National Endowment for the Arts, some of my compadres gave me a send-off that included a very nice engraved glass ice bucket which they filled with hot yellow liquid to float a tiny boat. The yellow liquid represented urine *al la* Andres Serrano's *Piss Christ* which I surely am not going to deal with in this book.

I am having a little trouble getting locked in here, but the purpose of this book is to articulate a personal philosophy of rowing—a Rowology if you will.

Rowology is not a school of philosophy seeking intellectual hegemony over all other schools of thought. There are schools of fish that could do better. But just in case you wonder what a school of philosophy looks like, take Naturalism as articulated by Ernest Nagel. To naturalists there is an order and organization in nature that encompasses all that is or that happens. (That includes just about the whole ball of wax.) This vast variety interacts "contingently", i.e., there is no guiding hand. Things just smash into each other randomly and stuff happens. In other words, "the furniture of the world" can be rearranged.

I don't know about you, but to view the meaning of life as the little woman rearranging the living room chairs works for me. All of this has to do with free will and human destiny (in fact the title of the great book of systematic theology written by my hero Reinhold Niebuhr is *The Nature and Destiny of Man*), but if you are ok with seats (like seats in a boat) I can slide into my summary of rowing and philosophy without you noticing I have skipped a few logical steps.

So here it is. I've got eight (what a happy coincidence since there are eight rowers in an eight) points to make and here they go.

NUMBER ONE

Efficiency. You can't win a race if you are not efficient. Fly and die. That is the fate of crews that go out too fast and can't sustain the pace. Life, rowing, and philosophy all share the virtue of efficiency. Not wasting time, energy, emotion, and happiness are virtues. Think of these lyrics by those great American philosophers, The Eagles: *You can waste all your time making money / You can spend all your love makin' time.*

Efficiency to me is getting maximum power out of each stroke; maximum benefit out of each thought; maximum enjoyment out of each day. We live in a universe of limited resources even if we who are blessed with abundance don't acknowledge it. If we don't use our talents, our resources, our opportunities efficiently, then we squander them and when they are gone they are GONE.

NUMBER TWO

Steadfastness. This is an old-fashioned, even biblical sounding word. What it means at its root is hanging in there. You can't quit 750 meters into a race. You owe it to your fellow crewmembers to die first. Woody Allen said that 95 percent of life is showing up, but that other 5 percent is a bitch. It means you are responsible, both to yourself and to others.

It means you finish what you started. It means no matter how terrible your case gets, how many witnesses go south, how hateful the judge's rulings, you hang in there because you owe it to your client and to yourself.

It means that even if you think every politician is a crook, every decision biased, every new law designed to benefit the least deserving, you do not give up on democracy because it is the only political system where hope is built in. You persevere because that is the way you are put together, that is the way you are trained and that is all you know how to do.

NUMBER THREE

Courage. There is a whole chapter later in this book about physical courage, but what I mean here is moral courage: doing what you know is right no matter what the personal cost. And there will be a substantial personal cost, believe me. Lost friends. Lost business. Lost opportunities. You have heard the saying: "To get along, go along." That is the moral philosophy of a salamander. Moral courage costs plenty. Going along is free. Here is what Ernest Hemmingway said about it:

"Moral courage is a rarer commodity than bravery in battle or great intelligence. Yet it is the one essential, vital quality of those who seek to change a world which yields most painfully to change" (*A Farewell to Arms*).

Moral courage is Martin Luther King, Jr. writing to his fellow (white) clergy and saying: "I am in the Birmingham jail because I am black. What are you going to do about it?" The answer, unfortunately, was, not much.

Moral courage is the home school parent, the animal rescue saint, the gardener who wants to reduce her carbon footprint. Moral courage isn't written in capital letters; it is a matter of everyday actions that consciously benefit others. It is not laughing at a racist joke, redoing a poorly done job, saying "I'm sorry."

Does rowing teach moral courage? No, not explicitly. But it does teach physical courage and the two are connected. Courage is the willingness to sacrifice for someone or something else. It is the spirit and the power that says: "This has to be done. I will do it." It is the selflessness that recognizes that no one of us is the center of the universe and that there are goals and causes greater than ourselves to be served. That is courage, be it moral or physical, and any life lesson that can teach it is valuable. So row on.

NUMBER FOUR

Being an amateur. What an insult. What a putz. Somebody who is a dabbler; a swell who has no talent. As David Halberstam recognized, rowers are the ultimate amateurs because there are no professionals. And bless the sport for that.

It was not always so. Toward the end of the nineteenth century, professional rowing was a major spectator sport and Edward "Ned" Hanlan, a Canadian from Toronto, was an acknowledged superstar. He won the world Professional Rowing Championship in 1880 and was adopted in the United States as an "American champion" and ultimate sports hero.

The previous year, on the Potomac in Washington, D.C., he raced before more than 100,000 spectators including President Rutherford B. Hayes and members of Congress (who adjourned from their lawmaking to watch him). Hanlan is reputed to have lost only six out of 300 professional singles races and at least three heroic ballads, along with saleable sheet music, were written about his exploits.

Artist Thomas Eakins painted the Biglin Brothers Rounding the Stake in 1872 (viewable today at the Cleveland Museum of Art). The brothers won the American Championship held at Poughkeepsie, New York in 1865, and since the crowd had wagered an estimated $100,000 on the outcome of this four-oared race, and the result was disputed, a near riot broke out. Professional rowing on the Chicago River harkens back to at least 1858 when the Metropolitan Rowing Club battled the Shakespeare Rowing Club of Toronto over a five mile course for a winner's prize of $1,000—a purse equivalent to a major golf tournament today.

Ironically, as rowing equipment improved (for example, wheeled carriages for the seat instead of a greased platform and leather shorts) boats and oars became more expensive, and at least in the United States, the increased interest in baseball, basketball and football left rowing literally in a backwater. It was rowing's good fortune to have thus been re-virginized into a purely amateur sport.

Amateur means a lover of the activity and you won't find a more romantic group than rowers. They do it because they love it and they work voluntarily (and we're talking real work here—lost skin, sore muscles and an occasional unscheduled throw up). When they are supposed to be doing other work, they fantasize about rowing because it is so compelling. That is an amateur all right: someone who is so consumed with a sport that it becomes a philosophy of life—a metaphor—a Rowology.

Let's see if we can put some component parts together: discipline, strength, compatibility, teamwork, aesthetics, fun, timing, control, power. Can you really harness all of that together and still be an amateur? Absolutely.

NUMBER FIVE

Transcendence. Or maybe you prefer the word spirituality? Both flirt with the sublime. Transcendence: to catapult out of the earth-bound to some cosmic venue; or spirituality where we cuddle up to the Almighty and bask in the glory of it all. What I have in mind is a little more mundane, but still it has some of the shimmery, frosted flakiness of the great beyond.

I'm talking about oneness with the water; oneness with my body; oneness with the universe. I'm thinking of motion that is continuous and seamless and fluid. I'm thinking of a mind that is completely focused and, paradoxically, completely at rest.

Either word—spirituality or transcendence—defines itself reluctantly. The concept is illusive, ever deepening, and ultimately unpossessable. We sense it, as the apostle Paul said, "through a glass darkly." Yes, I know Paul was not on the first string—the dream team—the starting twelve—of apostles, but in common parlance he is referred to as an apostle, so lighten up.

But they—it—the sensation is real and undeniably part of rowing whether in a single on flat water early in the morning when the rest of the city is still damp and groggy, or in an eight that has started magically to swing. (Swinging in rowing is the ultimate achievement where everyone in the boat is so attuned that every motion and every molecule is aligned.) Unfortunately this rarely happens, and when it does, you only recognize it after it is over. But when you have achieved the perfect catch where your oar grips the water and every ounce of your power flows through your body to propel the boat, then you are transported, both physically and spiritually. No kidding. Thing is, though, there is no time to pose and admire it like a golfer following his shot, because you have to do it all over again for the next stroke and the stroke after that and on into eternity.

There is a heightening of the senses here, most notable in a single, where you can feel every part of your body and the harmony of each stroke. You can close your eyes and sense the water, your balance as you come up the slide, your feet as you make small corrections in your course by pressing harder with one foot or the other. Remember to open your eyes before you crash into that snag. When Plato separated mind and body—well, he just hadn't done enough rowing, and anyway, when Plato was around, rowers were chained to their seats which had to make it less alluring—particularly when the boat capsized.

NUMBER SIX

Self-knowledge. You can't get it without pain. A trial lawyer mentor of mine said that he never learned anything from a case he won. That doesn't mean you try to lose a few just for the education, but it is true that life's hard lessons smack us upside the head. Those are the lessons that do not have to be repeated. Eleanor Roosevelt urged us to "learn from the mistakes of others. You do not have time to make them all yourself."

That is why I favor racing even if you aren't strong or experienced or don't foolishly crave medals (forget about attention—nobody else cares). Racing teaches us about ourselves; about our limitations and how we arbitrarily set them; about courage and how we seldom test it; about preparation and how we often neglect it. These are the lessons that show how plastic our lives are and how we can stretch and change and grow.

We humans are very good at fooling ourselves and we are in a constant state of flux. Hence knowing yourself requires both ripping off the multiple masks we wear, and also recognizing that who we are today is not likely to be who we are tomorrow.

Can rowing make you a better person or scholar? You bet. Mental toughness and mental discipline are not that different from their physical siblings. It is all one body, and self-awareness and self-evaluation come out of the same head.

NUMBER SEVEN

Celebration. We don't celebrate enough and that is a shame because it is one activity that brings us together and builds community. I'm not just talking about the jumping up and down and hugs and high fives and photos after the race. Celebration is in order on the nastiest day when it is cold and choppy and wet because it is a gift to just be out there doing something you love.

Celebration links up with the spiritual because we are thankful for what we have been given and what we have achieved together. We have created a bond and in that sense we know we are not alone and abandoned in the universe. We have made friends annealed together through common effort. So put that in your pipe and smoke it you depressing existential fatalists. One twentieth-century existentialist philosopher, whom I have chosen not to include in this book, is

Martin Heidegger who is quoted as saying: "making itself intelligible is suicide for philosophy." Philosophy, in my view, only makes sense if it makes sense. If it isn't useable, it isn't useful.

Number Eight

Aesthetics. Why do farmers plant flowers? Because humankind cannot live without beauty. "If you have but two pennies, buy a loaf of bread with one and a lily with the other." (I quote the last because I got it from somewhere—probably a famous philosopher.)

Rowing is infused with beauty from the shape and design of the boats to the grace and power of the sport itself. There is beauty in the motion without noise, in the flow of the boat through the water, and in being part of something that is somehow larger than our own lives.

There is beauty in the seasons as the willows along the riverbank quicken in the spring or the leaves color or the mist ebbs and flows as if it were alive. There is beauty in the banks where the salmon spawn and the beavers chew and the ducks hang out. There is beauty in weighing enough (stopping) to let a mother duck with her chicks in a line astern pass by. If you can't find beauty in all of that, check to see if you have a pulse.

While the focus of this book is on rowing—Rowology—its lessons are universally applicable. My brother Phil, who not only forged a wonderful career as a singer, but also was a beloved teacher and colleague to legions, contended that lessons of voice production, concentration, scholarship, musicianship, and determination are applicable to everything: business, farming, dunking a basketball, cleaning out the garage. "Good teachers," he said, "are all alike. Only the lingo is different."

So, in sum, does rowing solve the philosophical questions posed from time immemorial? It helps, but like so many questions, the answer depends on what framework, what life view, what baggage we bring. I think grabbing our preconceptions, shaking them by the scruff of the neck and making them earn their keep on the shelves of our minds is healthy—necessary even. The best way I have found to steam clean the brain is to row to exhaustion.

The Rowton

In the following chapters, the Rowton will speak, uttering wisdom or drivel. Think of the Rowton as your mother or your mentor or your conscience, or just as an uninvited wiseass. The unsolicited advice is free. It is taking or ignoring it that costs. Like many narrators in literature, the Rowton may be unreliable. Lots of the philosophers jumping off the page here spent lifetimes seeking to know themselves. But self-knowledge is ephemeral while self-delusion is constant. Maybe the Rowton is helpful, maybe not. On this proposition, however, the Rowton and I completely agree: if you spend too much time messing around in your head without getting out on the water and blowing out some of those negative ions, you are in big trouble. Nietzsche's Zarathustra, whom you will meet in this book, urges us higher types to learn how to dance. Why not?

I didn't invent the idea of an out-of-body inquisitor any more than James Cameron invented the Avatar in his movie. Nietzsche talked to himself through Zarathustra, a mythical mouthpiece fueled by opium, megalomania, and fanatical nuttiness. And yet, Nietzsche's four parts of *Thus Spoke Zarathustra*, as we will see later in this book, were, and still are, the touchstone for today's philosophers. You don't have to be crazy to be a famous philosopher, but some of the finest definitely were.

So what if the Rowton misleads us; so do professors, politicians, judges, parents, and priests. In fact, the most common characteristic of what we describe as higher intelligence is the ability to fool ourselves and others. Philosophy is the attempt to cut through all of the obfuscation (a polite word for BS) and hack out something that is meaningful. And that is why reading what the philosopher has written, rather than what someone else has written about him, is what I recommend.

You might therefore ask, "Why should I read your book?" Ask the Rowton.

Chapter 2

Why Philosophy?

> "Happiness, it turns out, is a destination we reach only when we are trying to get somewhere else." Matthew Syed

Philosophy teaches us how to think. It poses questions, examines responses, encourages us to save the persuasive and discard the frivolous, and gives us the tools to create our own game plan for living life. Philosophy is, arguably, the most important subject any of us could study at any stage of our lives and why it was so scary to me when I was in college is now a mystery. Actually, I do know. I thought one had to start with the hard stuff—the dialogues of Philo or Wittgenstein's puzzle theory. Those make your head hurt and explain why, in Aristotle's words, "beginners in philosophy despair." What I am suggesting is that we sneak up on philosophy, grab it by the tail and take it for a row.

I went to graduate school at the University of Chicago to sit at the feet of the famous theologian and philosopher, Paul Tillich. He died three weeks after I got there. Talk about rude. Life has that way of changing on us, of making sure we don't get too comfortable, of throwing sliders when we are looking for a curveball. But if you haven't practiced your logical skills, you will have about as much chance of doing well in life as a novice crew would have against an Olympic eight.

Clarity of Thought

That is what philosophy is about. How many times have we engaged in heated arguments, passionate arguments, noisy and sometimes drunken arguments without ever being clear what we are arguing about? What I have just described is an adequate definition of current American politics. Obviously there are no winners in such arguments.

Philosophy requires us to ask "why?" It invites us to peel back the onion skin one layer at a time, analyzing each new layer to see how it fits with the old, never being satisfied until enough makes sense to go on. Philosophy is systematic like mathematics in the sense that if 2+2 doesn't equal 4, then we don't have any basis for asking what 4+4 equals.

HABITS OF THE MIND AND MENTAL TOUGHNESS

Those are results from the study of philosophy and they are fundamental to the educated person and, I might add, to the successful person in any field of endeavor. These characteristics do not spring full grown from the forehead of Zeus. They are earned by study and inquiry and preparation and practice just as is the successful rowing stroke. Accurate fact gathering is a habit of both philosophy and the successful life.

But learning to think critically and accurately, to spot the baloney in any argument, to express yourself clearly and persuasively, those are just part of the package philosophy brings to the table. Who among us does not seek to be happy in this one and only life we are given? So if we seek to be happy, should we just hope for the best, or might we want to study the components of a good life?

Ethics is that study. It is the search for the good that everyone seeks to get out of life. Ethics focuses on happiness, on fulfillment, on how people can interact to reach their goals and live together, on what obligations we have beyond what the law demands, on how we make choices, evaluate our options and satisfy our desires. I don't for a minute suggest that these choices are self-evident or easy, but they are an unavoidable part of life, so why would we not train ourselves to make the best possible choices for ourselves?

The great thing about being a philosopher is that you don't have to buy a uniform. Everything you need is in your head waiting patiently to be put to your service. But we don't answer life's questions in a vacuum. We need assurance that our thoughts, our solutions, our reactions are reasonable and that is where studying philosophers, who have struggled with exactly the same questions for the entire course of human history, is instructive.

SOCRATES THE ROWER

We don't know he wasn't. He lived during the Peloponnesian War (about 432 to 403 BCE) and he fought, apparently with some valor and great endurance. The Greek's primary weapon was the trireme, a ramming boat with three tiers of oars on each side. The Spartans were fierce competitors whose whole social structure revolved around creating the most effective killers known to the ancient world. So Socrates may have pulled an oar. We could add that to the mythical status that his life has achieved. Because there are no direct sources, everything that we know or think about him comes from his disciples, the most famous of whom was Plato.

Socrates served, as every citizen of Athens was expected to, as a soldier and participated in the siege of Potidaea in 432 BCE, where (and this is one of the few facts upon which all chroniclers of his life agree), he demonstrated almost superhuman stamina. Stamina is to rowing as fuel is to fire.

Remember that the word philosophy is a combination of philo (lover) and sophos (wisdom). It was Socrates singular quest to live his life in the pursuit of wisdom. The god Apollo made him do it. The oracle was consulted to answer the question: Is anyone wiser than Socrates? Apollo came back with the answer: no. So Socrates, knowing that he was not wise and that the gods could not be wrong, questioned everyone and everything nonstop. He concluded that wisdom eluded craftsmen, poets, politicians, orators, and other famous teachers. Not surprisingly "men set upon him with fists and tore his hair out."

So what is the take away from Socrates the rower? Stamina, for sure, and living a life of constant reevaluation. Setting goals to try harder and aim higher. Knowing one's self and being true to what one believes while at the same time, being persuadable in the face of new evidence or better logic. Those rules will not just make each one of us a better rower, but a better person. Who knows, we might even be willing to die for our convictions. Should we emulate his arrogance? I think not so much.

Well, wait a minute. There is a distinction to be made here. Self-confidence is the inner arrogance that says "I will beat you" as you sit at the starting line. It is the quiet confidence that says I have erged (the Concept II rowing machine that, next to the rack, is the most exquisite torture machine known to man), and tanked (the on-shore tanks with fixed sliding seats, oar locks and mirrors so you can watch your rowing stroke in admiration or horror) and rowed thousands of miles and I know what I can do and I am about to prove it. That kind of arrogance is essential. It is the outward arrogance that annoys people. To be inwardly arrogant and outwardly humble, that is the trick.

WHAT SOCRATES HAD TO SAY WHEN THEY WANTED TO SNUFF HIM

Why did the political leaders of Athens want Socrates to drink the hemlock and die? They charged him with neglecting the Gods, or perhaps endorsing a few too many, and corrupting the young. I. F. Stone suggests that Socrates kept asking questions that poked holes in the arguments of all of those in power so that they felt stupid and naturally they wanted to kill him.

Politics may have had a hand in his downfall, because Athens had been fighting Sparta for thirty years (the Peloponnesian War) and had lost. The war was costly and demoralizing and near its conclusion in 404 BCE, democracy was replaced by the thirty tyrants, some of whom had interacted with Socrates as he went around bothering people. Because Socrates was continually asking questions about the perfect form of government, the nature and character of justice and the like, those who restored democracy in 403 BCE may have thought him a subversive.

At least they gave Socrates an opportunity to defend himself, and his student Plato preserved that defense for us. It is a brilliant apology for why we should study philosophy, but it is "in your face" to the extent that Socrates must have known he would be convicted. First he showed that politicians puff and bluster, but actually know nothing and because he admitted he knows nothing, he was wiser than they. Then he acknowledged that the poets were good with words but didn't know what they were talking about and thus were fools, and then he annihilated the poor craftsmen, who, while skilled in their professions, claimed expertise beyond what they knew and thus were ninnys. Good so far on winning over the jury.

Next he called one of his accusers an "impudent scoundrel" and showed that the accusation was self-contradictory, circular, and nonsensical. After all that, he wiped his hands together and said if he were convicted, it would only be because of the slander and malice of the crowd. If you are a trial lawyer and you want a model of how to lose, this is it.

But Socrates' defense is a moral manifesto and therein lies its power. Just as a soldier cannot flee the battlefield, so a philosopher can't abandon thinking because he fears death. He said his greatest gift to Athens was to persuade its citizens to seek wisdom, not wealth, and to encourage its leaders to value the soul of the city.

Socrates didn't win any points for humility in saying that he was a gift of God sent to the Athenians to help set them straight, but he was the very model of a life well lived. He demonstrated that he was willing to choose death over injustice. He said that if one truly wants to fight for justice, it cannot be done within the realm of politics. Liberty of the mind is the greatest good, and he would not weep or plead for mercy. The lesson, of course, is that no one can attempt to fix the world's problems without cost to himself.

Guilty, said the jury, but not by much. It was 500 persons strong and the vote, 280-220. The penalty was death but Socrates got to propose an alternative and, true to form, he suggested that he be given a lifetime of free meals at the Prytaneum, a building on the North slope of the Acropolis for honored guests and Olympic sports heroes. Death, cried the jury.

He drank the hemlock with great dignity and predicted that those who voted against him would not escape the judgment of history. The unexamined life, he said, was no life for a human being to live. Nothing can harm a good man—not in life or in death.

ROWTON

This is entertaining, but how can anyone know what he will do until actually faced with the crisis situation? Until then, courage is just a word.

One of my intrepid coworkers at the concrete pipe plant in Central Point, Oregon where I worked one college summer, was going to take life by the horns and thus bought a leather bound set of the Great Books that even came with its own book case. "They are all about Plato and Aristotle and them there fellers," he told me. He got screwed and those leather bindings were never cracked open, but there are life lessons there—lessons that do not change with technology or progress or wealth. Unfortunately for human kind they are lessons we never quite seem to learn.

CHAPTER 3

Why Row?

> "Poets utter great and wise things they themselves do not understand."
> Plato

To be able to look at yourself in the mirror and not be totally revolted; that's one reason. Rowing is the single best all-body exercise I know and because you can do it with others, say in an eight person shell where you can't just check out for a few minutes, it forces you to exercise more efficiently and more strenuously than you could on your own. Samuel Johnson, the eighteenth-century figure who knew about almost everything, wrote: "much happiness is to be gained, and...much misery escaped by frequent and violent agitation of the body."

We humans are communal beings and our team sports reflect that. Communities function, or not, depending on the amount of common vision, cooperation and sharing of the load. We are having a bit of a problem with this in America these days where the political parties get off on loathing each other, Congress can't even pass a budget, and when you ask a class what truths we hold self-evident (you know, like life, liberty and the pursuit of happiness in the Declaration of Independence), the best they can come up with is that people drive slowly in the fast lane.

But even the folks in a novice eight know the self-evident truths that the coxswain is in charge of the boat (she has the mic and the rudder), all the oars have to go into the water at the same time, you stop and go together, and if you don't play by the rules, you are likely to have your oar kick back, catch you in the chest and dump you out of the boat (this is called "catching a crab" about which there will be much hilarity later).

Rowing, like all competitive sport, entails a lot of pain. As one novice racer put it, he was sucking his heart out through his nose after 500 meters. But it feels so good once you stop. You can run up a couple of flights of stairs without breathing hard and you feel good all day. The endorphins that are released in the brain control your mood for hours afterwards. The brain, as Woody Allen put it, is his second favorite organ.

To race, and hopefully to win, that's another reason. If you say: "I am not competitive," I retort: "bullfeathers." You may not be competitive with a capital C like the trial lawyer I once faced who whispered obscenities to me and my spotlessly upright client when the judge wasn't looking, but you want your children to do well in school, you try to become a better cook, driver, husband, or gardener, and you enjoy getting a raise or a good performance review. The thing about rowing is that every stroke is an opportunity to do better, and every race is, too. If last race you finished DFL (dead, f-word, last), then fourth in your next race is cause for high fives all around.

ROWTON

Life is competitive. Not all that long ago, we were lunch for a saber tooth tiger and we only escaped that fate by learning to build structures, weapons and communities to protect ourselves.

If anything, humans as a species, are too competitive and that is why, over the span of my lifetime, there has been a war every six years. But just as free speech is a palliative that prevents us from hosing down our neighbor with an uzi, competitive sports channel our bloodlust to a more, dare I say, civilized venue.

Community keeps popping up here, and it is another, perhaps the most compelling reason to row. Where else can you be a seventy year old geezer and feel like you are back in college? Every three minute sprint race generates hours of conversation, and your other team members are buddies. In fact, at regattas it seems like everybody is friendly and helpful and happy. Would that the neighborhood of the world were so endowed. Many friendships are situational—sharing the same experiences, be it rowing, school, or the military. The context provides the permission and comfort for greater understanding and appreciation.

FOR ACCOMPLISHMENT

To travel across continents, spend thousands of dollars, and plan your life around trying to win a fifty cent medal is beyond compulsive, but I know I am not alone in this quixotic quest. Four ladies from Corvallis Rowing Club decided they would give it a go at Nationals, and in Tennessee they came in third. They erged all winter, hiked vigorously on off days, and came in second the next year. Then in Camden, New Jersey in 2009, THEY WON! I was in a pair race and crossed the finish line just behind them, and the radiance emanating from that boat could have powered the whole east coast. Was it worth it? You need not ask.

I row because I love to be on the water. I like the way it moves, the way it looks back at you, its opaqueness, its quiet mystery. One of my favorite quotes is from Kenneth Grahame's 1908 children's book *Wind in the Willows*: "Believe me, my young friend, there is nothing—absolutely nothing—half so much worth doing as simply messing around in boats."

Picture this. Six a.m. on a late summer morning. The sun is just coming up and the mist is rising off of the Willamette River in Corvallis, Oregon. Beavers have been at work witnessed by the barkless sticks that float by. The ducks are out including the cute little black and white butterball and the stately luminous green headed mallard. An osprey swoops by, plucks a fish out of the water, and with its shrill "beep, beep" cry, rotates the fish fore and aft to lessen the drag and heads for its nest atop a utility pole.

On another row, I witness the niftiest piece of flying I have ever seen in birddom. An osprey is dive bombing a bald eagle (bald used to mean white). Eagles prey on carrion, other bird's eggs, and any stinky carcass of opportunity. Osprey are fierce and territorial, if less than half the size. The osprey dives at the eagle again and again and each time the eagle veers off just in time, and then, just as the osprey arrives, the eagle does a 180-degree roll with talons up. The birds both retire and call it a draw. Where but on the river can you see that?

BIRD PHILOSOPHY

Benjamin Franklin wanted the turkey for the national bird, but he lost out to those thinking the bald eagle more elegant. The bald eagle is indigenous only to North America, although the colonists didn't know that then, and it does have a certain swagger, despite its dumpster diving culinary habits. But I think the primary reason the bald eagle is an appropriate symbol for America is that, unlike its cousin the golden eagle, it will continue to fly into the wind whether it is making any progress or not.

Poet Mary Oliver writes: "Whoever you are, no matter how lonely, / the world offers itself to your imagination, /calls you like the wild geese, harsh and exciting-- / over and over announcing your place / in the family of things." We can learn a lot from birds, and poets, too. Poets, after all, do philosophy with economy.

All ducks are called ducks, but a male duck is a drake. Oregon, where I row among the ducks, has more than twenty varieties of ducks including saxony, appleyard, ancones, northern pintails, mallards, and muscovy. Ducks belong to the same bird family as geese and swans (*Anatidae*), and according to duck champions, are more prolific in the egg department, more disease resistant, and more at home in the Oregon rain than chickens. The eggs taste the same (I am told). There is much more fascinating stuff about ducks including the corkscrew penis, but I am not going there.

Philosophy and Religion

Water is central to virtually all the world's religions, both because it is necessary for life, and because it symbolizes cleansing. At Buddhist funerals, water is poured into an overflowing bowl with the incantation: "As the rains fill the rivers…may what is given here reach the departed." Central to the Torah is the great flood in which God saved Noah for his faith and Noah saved the animals (and no, Joan of Arc was not Noah's wife). Christians baptize with water symbolic of washing away of sins, declaring faith and bonding with the community of believers. The King James Version of the Bible references water 363 times.

Hindus hold all water sacred, especially the Ganges River. The faithful make pilgrimages to sacred rivers to purify themselves. Likewise, Muslims purify with water before approaching Allah in prayer, before touching the Koran, and after sex.

The hymn line "peace like a river" acknowledges the soothing, calming, renewing power of water. Muslims have a particular genius for incorporating water into their architecture, as the Alhambra in Granada, Spain attests with astonishing beauty. But water can be hostile and destructive, too. I was in the Navy during the Vietnam War when the Tet offensive so unexpectedly arrived, and my ship turned around from its transit to Japan and hustled back to Vietnam at flank speed. We were chasing a typhoon and we caught it with green water coming over the bridge forty feet off the surface. My job was in the engine room and I listened to rivets popping and wondered if our World War II hull was any match for the anger of the sea.

A couple more reasons why I row include blowing the cobwebs out of my head and reducing stress. These two are related. Stress is a great crippler, performance inhibiter, and illness inducer. Stress typically comes from anxiety about the unknown, a seemingly overwhelming pile of tasks or problems facing us, or a sense that we do not control our lives. We never control much of our lives, though, so it is a matter of figuring what we can control, and emphasizing that.

When I was Chairman of the National Endowment for the Arts in Washington, D.C. it seemed like everybody was after me (some with good reason): the press, the artists, the conservatives, the liberals, the Christians, the car nuts. This was during the great national debate over censorship, obscenity, federal funding of the arts, and how much money Senator Jesse Helms could raise by exploiting the issue. I kept my sanity, barely, by rowing my lungs out every morning on the Potomac.

CHAPTER 4

Plato (circa 428–348 BCE)

> Give me a boat that will carry two / and we'll both row, my love and I.
> Folk song

Plato is the undisputed father of Western philosophy. He created its style of question, answer, rejoinder, and synthesis that we call dialogues. He taught in parables and was willing to let the student try to figure out what he meant without providing "the Answer." He started an academy that lasted for more than 300 years in which the life of the mind and the search for justice, truth, and beauty superseded all else. Twentieth-century philosopher Alfred North Whitehead said that the European philosophical tradition is nothing more than a series of footnotes to Plato.

The name Plato comes from the Greek word *platus* meaning wide. Perhaps it was his broad shoulders or wide forehead or prodigious mind that suggested the name, but more intriguing is his virgin birth, four centuries before Christ. The lore is that Apollo was his sire—which made him a divine man—who was a "fellow servant of the swans." He apparently had dreams of being a swan, but how that affected his thinking, I can't imagine. Suffice it to say that myth and reality blend into a picture of a commanding figure and a towering intellect.

I have absolutely no evidence that Plato said anything whatsoever about rowing. It's a shame really because he wrote about almost everything else: birth control, communism, socialism, feminism, vegetarianism, morality, politics, aristocracy, nature. And eugenics. Not any old yokels should be allowed to mate. Offspring of such unsupervised couplings should be left out in the weather to die. He was one tough customer. The closest to rowing I could find is that Dionysius the Younger, then ruler of Syracuse, sent a trireme (that rowing warship with three tiers of oars on each side) to fetch Plato from Athens—the equivalent today of sending your Lear jet. Presumably Plato was not required to row.

The separation of body and mind, with the emphasis on the latter, is attributed with some justification to Plato. It stems from his analysis of politics and how the community of humans should govern themselves. Plato had a deep distrust of the mob, stemming primarily from the conviction of Socrates and resulting death penalty. His political goal was to create the perfect ruler and the great unwashed in a democracy were definitely not it. We choose competent shoemakers, said he, but assume anyone who can get votes can rule a city. He had a point.

So, only a philosopher king is fit to rule. To prevent children from being corrupted by their elders, the first ten years should be primarily physical education. This was to be hard core training because indolence and luxury lead to farts (flatulence) and snot (catarrh). I have never seen it put quite so delicately.

Music was to be the leavening influence on athletes but none of that Barry Manilow cra... sorry, I am inserting myself as if I were a swan. Next, for those who pass the physical tests, is moral education and those who are best go on to philosophy where they are taught to think clearly (metaphysics) and rule wisely (politics). The goal of education is a search for compelling ideas that produce laws of sequence and ideals of development.

Then these educated philosophers go out into the world and work for fifteen years before they become fit to be "guardians" or rulers. Such a guardian could be of either gender, but would have no property and no spouse so as not to be distracted from the singular business of ruling wisely and well.

Plato favored the tyrant (although that term did not have such a negative connotation in his day). And he tried to make his politics happen. He figured if he could persuade just one tyrant to be a philosopher, he could create a political utopia. Thus he set to work on Dionysius of Syracuse. The court was filled with intrigue, plots and counter plots, misinformation, and accusation. Plato succeeded in insulting the powerful ruler with his unrelenting cross examination and was put under house arrest. He finally escaped, his noble experiment in tatters—wasted on an all too human pupil.

Although Plato continued to believe that philosophy might end the tribulations of self-interested human rule, the verdict more properly is that voiced by Callicles in Plato's dialogue, Gorgias: "Philosophers...are inexperienced in the laws of their city, inexperienced in the language to be used in business contracts..., inexperienced in human pleasures and desires, utterly inexperienced...in human character. So when they come to action...they make fools of themselves." It is an enduring and unfortunate condemnation of philosophy because the point of philosophy, of the inquiry into what is the good life, the just life, the life filled with beauty, is to be able to realize that life and live it.

We learn by experience and much of that experience consists of mistakes. We learn by analyzing how one part of our experience connects with other parts. We learn by asking questions and challenging what we think we know against what happens every day. There is no place in philosophy for the closed and armored mind. As Socrates put it, there is no greater evil than to hate reasonable discourse. Always welcome is the mind that is persuadable, and inquisitive and ready to row.

But Plato, in *The Republic*, takes a swing at the arts with which I would take issue. He says that in the ideal society all artists would be banned because they distort the truth. What they create is an image of an image, at least twice removed from reality and thus they are not just deficient in truth, but come from an inferior part of the soul. High slander, that. My belief is that artists, poets, singers, dancers present an alternative truth and they are in exactly the same business as was Socrates (in whose mouth Plato puts this libel): the business of making us think, making us see anew and decide for ourselves. Philosophy is the tool we use to justify our own thinking and any aid to that enterprise is welcome.

One of the reasons Plato is so relevant today is that he was reacting to a culture that acknowledged many gods. Unlike the monotheistic gods of Christianity, Islam and Judaism to come later in time, you didn't want to be noticed by these gods. You did your best to stay out of their way because if you displeased them they could seriously mess with you. Since morality has been dictated by the holy books and writings of the monotheistic religions for the last 2,000 years, and since many parts of the world are increasingly secular today, we can learn a lot from the intellectual free-for-all that preceded monotheism.

Chapter 5

Tools of the Trade

> "I disagree with what your lapel pin says, but will defend to the death your right to stick it." Apologies to Voltaire

It is a poor workman who blames his tools, but crappy equipment makes rowing so much harder. Let's start with the boat. A single scull for racing is about twenty-six feet long, a foot wide and weighs just over thirty pounds. Wing riggers are common and fit in back of the cockpit, flaring forward (or just the opposite if mounted in front of where the rower sits).

Obviously with a boat so long and narrow, you need the oars for balance. Sculling oars are about nine and one half feet long and have blades shaped like tulips, hatchets, cleavers, or other medieval weapons of mayhem. At the end of the rigger is the oarlock with a keeper on top to make sure the oar doesn't come out (because if it does, you are going swimming pronto). Grips are plastic or rubber, to be held in the palm and fingers with the thumb over the end. The inboard length of the oars requires that the sculler bring the left hand over the right when completing the stroke, otherwise the hands smash into each other causing foul language, abrasions and minimal forward progress.

The part that causes many novices to repair back to the bar, even in the morning, is that you actually tie your feet into what look like running shoes fixed to the bottom of the boat. Envision yourself hanging upside down underwater with your feet securely fastened, and the bar, by contrast, looks pretty good. When you go over, your feet come out. Trust me, I've tested it on purpose and accidentally many, many times.

The other oddity that discourages some is that you sit facing backwards. How do you know where you are going? Sometimes you don't. We ran into the Swedes at the World Games a few summers ago. Knocked our bow number off. The idea is that you look over your shoulder, or use a bike mirror, or watch the shoreline, or backsight on that tree way back there. You get used to it after a while, and in bigger boats, a coxswain does the steering and looking out for objects such as stumps, other boats, dead horses. Success here varies.

That brings us to the power part of the boat and that is the sliding seat, wheels that run in a grooved track or slide so you can bring your knees up to your chest, drop the blades into the water, and DRIVE with your legs—the strongest muscles in your body. It is the dropping of the oars into the water—the catch—where the perfect stroke starts.

Philosophical Point

Well, it isn't, actually. It is and it isn't. I don't know, really. The stroke is continuous motion with each part leading seamlessly into the next, and in this sense it is like the always popular philosophical issue of the chicken and the egg, which is a thinly disguised metaphor for whether God exists, which is to say that philosophy, and particularly ethics, is a logical progression, once you decide where to start, but that is the big problem because no one but those already convinced agree, and all of this makes my head hurt, anyway. Does that help?

Your single should fit you. I didn't know this for about fifteen years. I learned sculling in club boats and thought all boats were created equal. I got a good deal on a racing boat just as we left Washington on our way to Montana, and I bought an old wherry for Leah to row. (A wherry is a little wider and shorter, and theoretically more stable for beginning scullers.)

Digression

We set out for Montana in a Nissan pickup with a cap over the bed, the wherry and scull on roof racks I had made, and our monster dog, Annie in the back. We got a late start and at about dark pulled into a motel somewhere in eastern Pennsylvania. I went in to inquire and when I asked if I could see the room before we paid, the lady called for a guy behind the curtain who appeared shirtless with a baseball bat (Aluminum—an Easton, I think) which he was slapping in his palm. He said: "No dogs here, can't you read the sign." I said she could stay in the truck. "She's still a dog, ain't she?" And then he said, "Get the hell outta here," which I did with dispatch. I have never been so glad to have a vehicle start. Leah may have given him a single digit gesture as we pealed out; I'm not sure, but I hope so.

Rowton

He (Mr. Shirtless) was right, of course, she was still a dog. He made a pure ontological observation. Bless him.

Continued Digression

As we motored through Michigan, a guy coming the other way was so excited to see two rowing boats on top of the truck that he turned around, and chased us down so he could talk rowing. This was August, but as we approached the Montana boarder, the wind was blowing so hard that my homemade racks gave way and the boats started to slide off. I boosted Leah up and she managed to tie things together enough that we could limp in to Wibaux, where we had some great steaks and witnessed our first Montana dance. The kids drive a hundred miles for some non-bovine company.

Anyway, I rowed that single the only place I could around Bozeman, Hyalite Reservoir, elevation 7,200 feet. Take thirty strokes and your lungs cry for mercy. But where else can you see a bull moose grazing in the shore grass? With no one else who knew about sculls around, I didn't realize I was way too heavy for the one I bought. I rowed like a doofus because I couldn't get my oars off the water on the recovery. An analytical philosopher type person should have figured that out in fewer than fifteen years.

Philosophical Whiz-bang

My problem was under thinking, but lots of times over thinking blocks our solution just as dragging the oars over the water on the recovery slows the boat and ruins the run. Ideas need time to percolate and often the solution to a thorny problem pops into my mind when I am not thinking about it, but am just rowing along. We routinely drag our mind's oars on the recovery by forcing our thoughts into a pattern or demanding our minds be consistent. Our brains are scruffy and unfocused and the real stuff of genius is the ability to make connections between ideas that seemingly are completely unconnected. One of our most profound national thinkers, Thomas Jefferson, exercised wild ideological promiscuity because he was always looking for connections. He was not, to my knowledge, a rower. He did, however, suggest, with substantial justification, that the books in the Library of Congress be organized under the general headings of memory, reason and imagination.

I now row a Hudson elite heavyweight single that is as fast as it is beautiful. It fits me and allows me to get the catch ahead of the pin. That means that your body is fully compressed with your knees against your chest, arms fully extended and torso canted so that your blade drops in as far toward the bow as possible. The pin is the vertical metal piece at the end of the rigger against which all the pressure of the oar is placed. The more water each stroke moves, the faster you go. Actually, the water doesn't move. It provides the resistance and the boat moves. Each stroke leaves a whirlpool and the more cavitation, the harder you are pulling.

Philosophical Interlude

Why does it matter if the boat is beautiful? It matters a lot to me because beauty and craftsmanship go together in creating a superior product. Aesthetics, or the philosophy of beauty, investigates what makes beauty beautiful. Notwithstanding the dodos that attacked the output of the National Endowment for the Arts when I was Chairman, there are those who have spent lifetimes studying aesthetics, and it is not random walk. Individual tastes will vary but in every arts discipline there are standards and acknowledged masters of the craft.

The true test of art, particularly public art, is time. Take for example *La Grande Vitesse*, the Alexander Calder red metal stabile that was commissioned as one of the National Endowment's first pieces of public art in 1966. It arrived in a large public square in Grand Rapids and some of the denizens were less than thrilled: it's ugly, it's big and red and lumpy, it's in the way, a waste of money, goober, goober, goober. Fifty years later there is a festival around the sculpture, it is the City's logo, it is on the stationery, the sides of the garbage trucks—it is, in a word, beloved. Similarly, the audience in Paris booed the premier of Bizet's *Carmen* but it has managed not just to endure, but to be the only opera many people know.

It gives me great pleasure every time I take my Hudson off the rack, every time I put it in the water, every time I dry it off. One can do worse than to live surrounding one's self with beauty, and if the beauty is functional, all the better. Next time you are in Washington, D.C., stop by the National Gallery and admire the painting by Auguste Renoir entitled *Oarsmen at Chatou*—beauty and utility, indeed.

I have described only the single scull, but there are pairs (two rowers, one oar each—the hardest boat to row well), doubles (two rowers, two oars each), fours with or without coxswain (one oar per rower), quads (four rowers, two oars each), and eights (one oar per customer, and always a coxswain). No grand philosophical theorem ties all of these craft together except that just as philosophy is about how people use ideas, rowing is about how people use both their minds and bodies. And rowing and philosophy share Goethe's admonition: "Nothing is more terrible than ignorance in action."

Remember the wherry I bought for Leah to learn in?* We took it up to Hyalite, got her launched, and she got the hang of it right away—not the full slide, full power part, but enough to make the boat go. The boat also began to leak. I was in my single and it was pretty clear Leah was going to be in the water even if she stayed upright, which she didn't. Then the issue was how to get boat and wife to shore. We did this by Leah clinging to the stern of my boat with her feet wrapped around the bow of the wherry. She kept getting detached from one boat or the other, having had little practice at being a tow rope, but we got to shore with only mild hypothermia. She has not rowed the wherry since.

*This isn't a footnote, but I want you to know that I know you are not supposed to end a sentence in a preposition. It is like the child who asked his mother to read to him and when she brought up the wrong book, he cried: "Why did you bring the book I did not want to be read to out of up for?" If you don't get it, see me after class.

CHAPTER 6

A Commercial for Philosophy

> "We're all so damn busy choppin' wood, we don't have time to sharpen the axe." Abraham Lincoln

To value philosophy is to value yourself. It expands our minds, our knowledge, and our confidence just as physical training expands our lungs, muscles and endurance. Here are ten reasons why this is so. You may agree with only two of them, or you may think of fifteen more, but either way, philosophy makes a compelling case for itself.

NUMBER ONE

Philosophy can free us from our prejudices and misconceptions. This is what Socrates was doing in response to the arguments of his fellow Athenians. He conceded that this little exercise at their expense annoyed them, but few prejudices and even fewer misconceptions can withstand cross-examination. You might say that prejudices are by their very nature irrational and emotional. Exactly. Reason and logic are the cleansers and antibacterials. Scrub a prejudice with a little powdered reason and it may go away—if you can get the bigot to stand still long enough to listen.

NUMBER TWO

Philosophy helps us spot and uncloak false arguments. It contains what scientist Carl Sagan called a baloney detector. Because we are bombarded with electronic messages nonstop, we have to have the tools to decide for ourselves what is true and what is not.

NUMBER THREE

Philosophy gives us food for the mind. Nobody is infallible and infallibility is not what philosophy gives, either. It doesn't give intellectual certainty, but rather intellectual confidence. This confidence allows us to defend our arguments, beliefs, and ideas. We may be proved wrong by a more compelling argument and in that case, philosophy gives us (we hope) the wisdom to see that we are wrong and the grace to accept it without fisticuffs.

Number Four

Philosophy teaches us to love learning. The most depressing admission about higher education in the United States today is that students are paying for a degree, not an education. The only education worth having is one in which we learn to educate ourselves, and for that to happen we have to love learning. I can remember when I fell in love with my wife, but not when I fell in love with learning. It snuck up on me. It is illusive, but some of its siren songs are identifiable: wondering what is in that new book; puzzling over a math proof while watching the dryer spin; realizing it is three o'clock and you missed lunch because the book was so compelling. Yep, you are in love, sucker. May it last a lifetime.

Number Five

Philosophy teaches that knowledge is aerobic—it is a pursuit but never a destination.

Number Six

Philosophy teaches us to live with uncertainty. Bertrand Russell says that philosophy's value is primarily in its uncertainty because it expands our thought, allows us to consider the possibilities and frees us from the "tyranny of custom." Uncertainty is the wet wood of thinking—hard to kindle. Students want to know *the* answer; they wave their hands and whine "is this going to be on the test?" Uncertainty is an acquired taste for sure, but it is also the way life is.

Number Seven

Philosophy keeps alive our sense of wonder by allowing us to approach familiar issues from new directions. Often this can happen simply by restating the issue or redefining the terms. By the way, reliable studies show that thinking creatively will also help you live longer, if you care.

Number Eight

Philosophy is calming because when we contemplate the really big issues like is there a God, and if so, how can She stand humankind, or what is truth, beauty or justice, we free ourselves from the petty everyday concerns of what's for dinner, can we pay the mortgage, and why is the sheriff knocking on the door. Calm abiding is like concentrated meditation which is like single mindedness. Each of these represents the "executive control" function of our brains so that we are able to put aside distractions and really focus. If you are grabbing for your phone every time it tickles you, forget about executive control because your mind is sweeping floors and pumping gas.

Number Nine

Philosophy teaches us that the right question is more important than the right answer.

Number Ten

Philosophy teaches the limitations of the human mind. Philosopher Ludwig Wittgenstein used to whack his stick on the ground in frustration when he could not get his mind around a thought he was trying to crystallize. The human mind is not meant to be governed. It works in unknowable ways and at unexpected times and often simply refuses, chucking us over the head of the horse and into the un-jumped jump.

Number Eleven

There should be either ten, like the commandments, or twelve like the apostles, but this is eleven, namely, that philosophy keeps us grounded. Grounding is not good for boats. Avoid it. But for humans on land, it is what we must have to deal with life's little spitballs. Philosophy has the huge advantage of allowing us to think about issues before we are in crisis. "Who am I?" "What do I stand for?" "How do I determine the truth?" "What am I prepared to die for?" And a whole bunch of other issues, most of which we will not have thought through before we are in the swamp. But philosophy will have given us the intellectual tools to forge an answer for ourselves. It may be, and in fact many times will be wrong, but at least we will not be defenseless in the face of a confusing and arbitrary world.

Let us not define the good life as the easy life here. The questions can be terrifying and the puny answers we devise, transitory. It took me forty-five years of off and on struggle to finally say out loud that I do not believe in God. I actually think I am closer to an agnostic than an atheist—I simply think humankind cannot know and that all of the stuff about revelation is manmade. But the other day at a museum I was looking at a medieval painting of judgment day and the different directions humans were going, and I thought, "what if it's true?" The answers that satisfy us today may not do the trick tomorrow or next week or next year, but at least they are answers we have sought and found. The alternative is to float along and to realize at some point that what we have lived is not our life.

CHAPTER 7

Aristotle (384–327 BCE)

"Roe v. Wade is not an alternative way of crossing the Potomac." Anon.

Aristotle conferred a lasting gift on us by embracing the link between science and philosophy. He favored mathematics and geometry, and taught that we can know the true nature of a thing by examining it, by gathering evidence, analyzing that evidence and drawing conclusions. This served not just scientific inquiry, but the discipline of logic, which he fairly can be said to have created. *Roe v. Wade* is the always and still controversial 1973 US Supreme Court abortion case.

As you are sitting there in your chair wondering why the hell you are reading Aristotle and not enjoying a brew at the corner tavern with your friends, Aristotle pops up and gives you *the answer*, the reason he wrote Nicomachean Ethics: it is about how to be happy. Aristotle was all over the pursuit of happiness long before Thomas Jefferson enshrined it in the Declaration of Independence.

We know next to nothing about the life of Aristotle. The twentieth-century German philosopher Martin Heidegger quipped: "The man was born, he worked and then died." Nicomachean is not a flavor of ethics; it is the name of Aristotle's son who, after his death, compiled Aristotle's works from his notes. Aristotle said that to do well and live well is to be happy and that is the goal of ethics. What an astonishing concept. Rather than ethics being a bunch of rules and prohibitions and roadblocks to what you want to do in life, it actually is a methodology to help us be happy. But it gets even better.

Aristotle championed reason in action (as opposed to pure reason which more characterizes some of Plato's dialogues). He specifically identified sport: "As in the Olympic games it is not the most beautiful and strongest who receive the crown, but those who actually enter the combat—those are the ones who win what is noble and good in life." You gotta suit up. Moreover, happiness is not something divinely bestowed. It comes to those who study, who pursue virtuous goals, who are steadfast and bear up under all of life's challenges with dignity and courage.

He describes three basic human endeavors: making, doing and thinking and then analyzes the kind of "productive thinking" needed for the first, the "practical thinking" for the second and the "speculative thinking" for the third. So from a rowing perspective, how you approach the perfect catch will differ from how you tackle truth or goodness. Man the doer, in this case the rower, has to have a specific end in view. A goal. It may be as short term as winning a seat race in today's practice or as cosmic as winning the women's 8+ at the next Olympics. Or it might be simply to be the best rower your unique body and mind will allow.

For Aristotle, the unplanned life is just a mess—not worth the bother. But your life plan has to be the right plan, the one that produces a virtuous life. He requires that we seek out and obtain the goods we need, in the right proportion, and learn the moral virtue to use those material goods and our bodies properly. The ultimate value of life depends on awareness achieved through the power of contemplation. Living well, not just surviving is the goal. And friendship, particularly in youth and old age, is a major part of the equation.

Moral virtue is the result of habits. We become virtuous by doing just acts, that is, by practice. Virtue doesn't arrive by chance or accident; it is the result of a person choosing deliberately to do a righteous act for its own sake. "We must take the oar if sailing is impossible." Rowing as a metaphor for the deliberately chosen moral life. Lovely.

How does one figure out what is virtuous? The soul arrives at truth by five means: art, science, prudence, wisdom and intuitive reason. Loss of self-control is a failure of character because prudence measures all things and seeks all things in the proper measure. Watch and analyze what a virtuous person does. Get a role model or a mentor. And remember, happiness requires not just diligent study, but also leisure.

Now having read this, do you know how to be happy? Bully for you if you do, but I suspect if you really read Aristotle, you know that it is a pursuit that will require a lifetime of dedication. But hey, isn't being happy worth it?

Comparing Plato's search for the exact form of an idea, and Aristotle's method of close observation and experience, we see what is a continuing division of philosophers to this day: the rationalists on the one hand and the experientialists on the other. Similarly, a division exists between the absolutists, and again Plato would fall into this category, and the relativists who believe that the form of an idea depends on the society from which it comes. (The pre-Socratics, and particularly the Sophists were relativists and were the targets of many of Plato's dialogues.) We can get a pretty good foundation in philosophy by comparing the form and content of Plato's thinking with that of his pupil, Aristotle.

CHAPTER 8

The Stroke

> "A man with no philosophy in him is the most inauspicious and unprofitable of all possible social mates." William James

Whether done consciously (as Aristotle urges) or accidentally, we devise a system of truths that give us guidance for how to interact with our fellow human beings. Philosophy seeks these truths purposely. It can start with a holy book such as the Bible, Koran, or Torah, with a reverence for nature as in many Native American religions, from observation of how things work in the natural world (like David Hume's pool balls hitting each other), or from about anywhere else that gives a basis for subsequent observations. Thoughts are tools, and so is an oar. It is the simplest of tools: an elemental and some would say primitive lever.

The rowing stroke is usually broken down into four parts for understanding, analysis and practice. Since the stroke is continuous and we have to start somewhere (just like philosophy), let's start at the release. This is where the power ends, your legs are fully extended, your body is leaning back slightly toward the bow (remember you are facing backwards), and the oar is almost to your chest. (We are in an eight here and you are either rowing port—the left side of the boat facing the bow—or starboard—the other side. The pointy end in the front is the bow, and in the back, the stern.)

Sweep oars are built so that they only work on one side of the boat. They are made of carbon fiber and the handle is either about eighteen inches of tapered wood, or two rubber or plastic gripping areas separated by a short shaft. You hold it with both hands, the inner hand turning the oar to feather it so it is horizontal to the water on the recovery, and the outside hand tapping it out of the water and serving as the primary connection between you and the oar on the power part of the stroke.

So you have tapped the oar out of the water at the end of the power part of the stroke. Now you smoothly push your hands away from your body, lean your torso from slightly toward the bow to slightly toward the stern (this is called body over, with your hips acting as the hinge and your arms holding the oar straight out in front of you), then you slowly begin to ease up the slide by bending your knees until they almost meet your chest, and then you drop the oar into the water by raising your hands ever so slightly and simultaneously drive your legs down flat gradually swinging your torso toward the bow. That's all there is to it—release, arms away, body over, slow slide, catch and drive. Sounds easy. Isn't.

David Hume, Scottish philosopher of the eighteenth-century thought that if we could just find a few common principles that were verifiable, we would have a foundation to give us guidance in morals and in understanding humankind and our passions. Every rowing coach is looking for the same thing—like breaking down the stroke into its elemental parts.

For Hume, it was not reason, but experience that gave a verifiable basis for understanding life. The pool ball example is that if one ball hits the other straight on, it will transfer energy to the inert ball. This can be demonstrated over and over and thus must be true. By similar observation, we can predict cause and effect in human interactions. For example, if one child hits another, he is likely to get hit back.

Hume wrote his *Treatise on Human Nature* before he was thirty. It was not a bestseller. In his words it fell "deadborn from the press." Not one to be easily discouraged, Hume anonymously wrote a pamphlet to decode and explain his treatise to the unwashed. This didn't work either, at least not for 200 years, until 1938 when the economist John Maynard Keynes discovered it and Hume leapt gleefully from the grave to illuminate morals, passion and human understanding.

Hume was on to something else that only by sophisticated neuroscience can we now prove in the twenty-first century: passion mugs reason. Functional magnetic resonance imaging, fMRIs, along with infrared spectrometry and a host of other sophisticated techniques that follow blood flow and chemicals in the brain have begun to unlock the secrets of how our brains actually function. It is clear that the old lizard brain, what Hume called passion, dictates our course and our "reason" makes up arguments to justify what we have already done. As Hume wrote: "our imagination has a great authority over our ideas."

Hume was also willing to give a sucker a break in not requiring perfection from those trying to live a moral life. He said we should not criticize a laudable action because there is a "tincture of vanity" in it. Vanity, he said, is closely allied with virtue and the two are almost impossible to separate. I take this to mean that it is alright to like yourself.

WILD DIGRESSION

The seven deadly sins have long been the no-nos of some moral philosophy, but I think they (the deadlies) have gotten a bad rap. In case you don't have them tattooed on your arm, they are pride, gluttony, anger, sloth, covetousness, envy and lust. If you want a mnemonic device to help you remember them it is: Presbyterians gasp at sight of crowds enjoying life.

The Greek word for pride is meglopsychia—largeness of soul. For Aristotle, life was about knowing one's self, trusting one's self and being satisfied with one's self. So when Muhammad Ali declared: "I am the greatest," he was just telling the truth. Aristotle would applaud.

And what's wrong with envy? I envy those who play the piano well, who emerge unscathed from a sand trap, who speak Italian to waiters. Envy is a positive force when it inspires us to do better or teaches us how to succeed. Envy only becomes toxic when we are consumed with what we cannot change, like growing old (which, by the way, I refuse to acknowledge).

As for anger, I think we need more, not less, but constructive anger that makes us get involved in our children's failing schools or be a part of the solution to quality health care for all. Positive anger holds our elected officials' feet to the fire. If we aren't angry, we aren't paying attention.

Covetousness and greed are used interchangeably and greed is easier to spell so I will use it (call it sloth on my part). Greed has gotten us into trouble lately, what with credit default swaps and all. The trick is knowing when enough is enough. Do we need five Ferraris when perhaps four would do? Moderation is both an ethical imperative and—surprise, surprise—the most satisfying.

Lust. Unfortunately what I remember about Jimmy Carter's presidency is his confession that he looked at women other than his wife with lust in his heart. Big deal. Without lust, the human race is toast.

What's left? Sloth. Doing nothing. Watching the world go by. With our frantic rate of consumption, sloth may be the only way to save the planet. Warning: sloth does not work for rowers.

Finally, gluttony. Gluttons were once much admired—Falstaffian characters full of wit and good cheer. But now with two thirds of us offending the scales, gluttony seems to have gained such incumbency as to be too common for special notice in the sin department. One reason for rowing is that if you row hard, you can eat anything you want.

Philosopher Joke

A philosopher and a historian are talking at a nudist camp and the philosopher asks: "Have you read Marx?" The historian replies: "Yes, I think they are from these wicker chairs."

This chapter is about the rowing stroke and I got distracted by Hume and deadly sins, but that is sort of the point. Philosophy is about life and life is about philosophy. The rowing stroke, as simple as it may seem, is infinitely complex and that is why we practice that stroke over and over and over. Similarly, we will never reach the perfect state of philosophical equipoise where we have done all the thinking we need to do. We must continue to think and observe and reevaluate—yes practice—in a fluid and very tricky universe.

One more observation about the rowing stroke: you can't make the boat go faster when your oar is out of the water, but you can make it go slower. One of the drills we do it to take our feet out of the stretchers (shoes in the bottom of the boat). Rowing this way means that you have to go up the slide by bending your knees rather than pulling yourself up by your feet. Why does this matter? Because you are sitting backwards and pressure on your footboard is against the motion of the boat. See, in both rowing and philosophy not all truths are self-evident. In fact most of them aren't.

CHAPTER 9

Courage

> "Courage is not simply one of the virtues, but the form of every virtue at the testing point." C.S Lewis

Socrates was a man of peace who taught Plato. Plato separated the mind and body, concentrating on the former while teaching Aristotle. Aristotle rejected the mind/body division and concentrated on the empirical world—what we can see, analyze and prove—while teaching Alexander the Great. Alexander, by the time he was twenty-five, had conquered most of the known world. He was a man of action.

ROWTON

And your point is...?

So what does the fact that Alexander wielded a mighty sword have to do with you sitting there in number three seat 600 meters into a sprint race thinking your head is going to explode? It's just that life shrinks or expands in relation to the chances we take, the challenges we meet, the failure we risk.

Granted, the magnitude of challenge may differ. We are not likely to see a headline: "Oregon State Crew Conquers Persia." But that is a difference of scale, not of kind. Conquering Persia and beating Cal require the same type of courage, the same type of mental preparation, the same kind of physical and emotional toughness.

Some rowers I know were at their first big race, which just happened to be the National Championships. Before the race they told a long-time coach: "We just want to get a medal." The coach did that little coach thing that they do when they know you are just cannon fodder, and wished them good luck knowing they had no chance. They weren't ready. They weren't mentally tough. They didn't have their game faces on.

Marcus Garvey, the great Negro leader in the early twentieth century said: "If you have no confidence in self, you are twice defeated in the race of life. With confidence, you have won even before you have started." While confidence and courage are not exactly the same, they share the willingness to leap into the fray. Whether you jump down from the parapet into a host of enemy swordsmen and smite them, as did Alexander, or line up for a race wishing you had hadn't had that last pancake is the difference between the prepared and the bewildered.

Aristotle, as scary as he seems, is really a pretty clear writer. He wanted us to be keen observers of the world, to catalogue the evidence we find, and then to analyze it in accordance with his four causes. Those are: what is the thing made of (the material cause); what is its pattern or model (the formal cause); how did it get here (the efficient cause); and what is it for (the final cause). This seems like elementary scientific method. Duhhh. He invented it and changed the course of Western, and probably world, history.

Aristotle thought and wrote about most everything including courage. Courage is a virtue, but to understand it, it must be analyzed in relation to two corresponding vices: cowardice and foolhardiness. Cowardice is refusing to suit up; pretending that life is meant to be easy; not confronting problems, personal demons, thorny issues. Foolhardiness is rejecting the reality of fear; pretending immortality; endangering others for one's own vain-glory. Courage falls somewhere between the two.

"We will either find a way or make one." So said Hannibal of Carthage on his way to tussle with the Romans in the Second Punic War. Courage has several helpmates: inventiveness is one, and discipline is another.

I'll bet you can hardly wait for me to try to shoehorn all of this into a rowing parable, but it actually is pretty elementary. The crews that win the races are the best prepared mentally and physically. They KNOW they are going to win—expect to win, are honked off if they don't. They have, to a person, the courage to row through the pain; to banish the negative thoughts during a race; and to keep concentration no matter what happens. Much of what we call courage is really the result of preparation. The army calls it training; coaches call it practice. The end goal of both is to be able to react to any situation without thinking.

COACHING DIGRESSION

The legendary track coach and cofounder of Nike, Bill Bowerman was a lifelong friend of my father Otto (sometimes known as Toot for reasons that need no explanation). The way Bill put it was: "You can't do the long jump without getting sand in your shorts." Like all good coaches, he expected you to produce far beyond what you thought you were able. But he wasn't beyond a few shenanigans. He and my father would pass cards under the table in their shoes when playing bridge against his wife Barbara and my mother MarAbel. One morning before church, Bill sewed a white thread through the lapel of his blue surge suit, leaving the rest of the spool in his inside pocket. After Barbara had pulled about three feet of thread out they were both laughing so hard they had to leave the sanctuary. He spotted a runner coming late to practice because of a dentist appointment. He called him over, said: "Open up; let me see," and popped in a worm. When he did a toot, he would slug you and yell "farts."

PHILOSOPHICAL RECAP

Courage comes in at least three flavors: physical courage (which includes the mental courage to keep the body going), moral courage where we dare to bear the cost of doing what we know is right , and learning courage, where we willingly expand our minds, set aside our assumptions and prejudices, and dare ourselves to grow. As Sir Edward Hillary put it: "It is not the mountain we conquer, but ourselves."

CHAPTER 10

Augustine (354–430 CE): The Rake, the Saint, and the Genius

"The greater the pain, the greater the gain." Ignatius of Antioch

Augustine was a mental, not a physical athlete. His angst filled writings, of which volumes survive, show an early life during which he flirted with, or even dated, Cicero's rhetoric, Manichaean Gnosticism, Skepticism, Neoplatonism and a wealth of other pagan or Christian beliefs before he embraced St Paul. During this intellectual odyssey he was womanizing and generally living high on the hog so that when he finally got the call from God, he said, "take me, but not yet." In due course he was appointed Bishop of Hippo (Northern Africa) and his writings became the template for Catholicism throughout the Middle Ages.

As a searcher during his entire life, Augustine concluded that reason alone is insufficient to explain life's riddles and, in fact, reason alone can lead one astray (using his own life as proof). Therefore, to be truly happy, one must be a part of a unified community of faith and must surrender to the authority of that community. The community can and should use political and spiritual coercion to keep people's thought right and curb free will (which leads to sin). For example, he said that while killing is prohibited, God grants special license ("an explicit commission") to an individual for a limited time when killing is God's will.

Because of his lifetime of inquiry and his failure to find "the answer," Augustine decided that what we can know is constrained. Most particularly, we can never truly know ourselves. We must look to the Church to answer those questions where the answer cannot be demonstrated by reason. He wrote: "Seek not to understand that you may believe, but believe that you may understand." A quiet mind is the reward of faith, he wrote, but those who put their faith in man are cursed.

It doesn't take a student of history to see the connection between this world view and the political and spiritual structure of Western Europe for the next 1,000 years. Scholars can debate whether it was good or bad (it was both), but Augustine's influence surpasses most in the history of the world.

We can, through the lens of history, appreciate Augustine's genius. But that doesn't tell us how a genius is made. A recent book contends that the whole idea of genius is over rated and that any ordinary yokel can, after practicing 10,000 hours, play the piano like Van Cliburn.

The proposition is utter drivel. Mozart was writing symphonies when he was four years old. He had hardly been out of the crib for 10,000 hours, let alone practiced that long. Genius is genius. Step aside and admire it. Praise it. Honor it and give thanks if you have it, but forget about copying it. It just won't happen.

Genius is rare. Mozart was a genius. Einstein was a genius. Edison was a genius, probably. You can add to the list, but it sure won't fill the phone book of the tiniest town.

I knew a guy, a client in fact, who was a financial genius. He understood money—how it works, how it multiplies, what its properties and rules are—the whole ball of wax. He had a jet, owned a bank, and had millions of dollars. He went to jail. That is, no doubt, a cautionary tale, but don't worry about it unless you, too, are a financial genius. And then, try to avoid selling the same mortgage to more than one person.

It strikes me that his knowledge was so complete and his grasp of finance so instinctual, that maybe he was guilty of nothing more than being much, much smarter than the judge in money matters. It's sort of like the Athenians sending Socrates to the promised land because he knew more than they. But while my client's understanding may have been virtual, his jail cell was totally actual.

Genius has an element of fairy dust about it. It isn't quantifiable. You can't hold it in your hand, and if you mistreat it, it will take a powder, both literally and figuratively.

Tiger Woods was the best known athlete in the world and was as close to a sports genius as anyone I can think of. Sure he had a father who was a constant teacher and demanding task master who would talk in his backswing, who coached and prodded him, and who groomed him for greatness. But he also had all the tools—the fierce concentration, the killer instinct, and the raw ability. His genius was in shot making where he was fearless. He hit shots mortals cannot copy, and he hit them when he had to. He played through pain and he won and won and won.

Then he crashed. Seldom has a public figure self-immolated as did he, and it is not my purpose to speculate why, or to wag a finger, or write a eulogy. My point is that he lost his genius and he may never get it back.

In tournaments since he has returned to the tour, he has not managed the killer close. He hasn't made the crucial approach or sunk the winning putt. He now is just one of the guys out there on the tour, all of whom are richly talented, but no longer is he the MAN among boys. Genius has fled and fickle mystery that it is, it cannot easily be recaptured.

So what does all this have to do with Augustine and with philosophy? Augustine might say that the mystery is that of God's grace and that it is the hubris of man that gets in the way of implementing God's plan through the teaching of the church.

Nietzsche, as we will see, would have liked Tiger since he exhibited the characteristics of the superman. In a rough sense the superman and the genius are in the same ball park. There are many different models of genius. Franklin Roosevelt, maybe in the political realm. Thomas Jefferson, absolutely.

Philosophy's job is to make sense out of life, so it is not a surprise that philosophy would want to investigate those that have extraordinary abilities. Plato's philosopher king was not a genius because the philosopher king reached that position only after a lifetime of training. Candidates spent years in preparation, were screened and vetted and only after a lifetime of grooming were they allowed to serve (in Plato's imagination). A genius just pops up and does it.

The genius has an incredible drive to succeed at what he or she does and that constant practice, rehearsal and dedication lasts a lifetime, or at least it lasts as long as the genius fairy hangs around. The philosophical equation is: the more talent you have, the harder you have to work.

What about luck? While luck may dictate the bounce of a fumble in football or the lipping out of a putt in golf, luck has very little to do with who wins a rowing race. Yes, equipment may break, but that happens seldom. Yes, one lane may get more of the wake rebound from the shore, or be more exposed to the wind, but for the most part, you win or lose because you are faster, stronger, and better trained. Period.

Then there is the luck of the draw. What talents were you bestowed with out of the womb? If your parents were Andre Agassi and Steffi Graf, you were probably born with a tennis racket in your hand. But if your parents were Fred and Wilma Smith, you better just suck it up and get on with things because there is not a lot you can do about it. No excuses, said Sartre. It is up to you to do the best you can. Some of the existentialists we will meet later in this book say we live in fear. Fear of being different, of not living up to what society expects of us, fear of change, fear of being creative. They say: "Chomp down on this bitter pill of life, masticate the hell out of it, and digest it." (That is my rough translation from the French, a language with which I am totally unfamiliar.)

Rowton

Then there are those who justify the existence of luck as the reason for the success of those they do not like.

CHAPTER 11

Anatomy of a Race

> "Luther Motts, founder an' president o' the Fit-at-Fifty Club dropped dead with his skates on." Kin Hubbard

Races are opportunities for great glory and total embarrassment. Thing is, you never know which one you are signing up for. But before we proceed, let's describe the kinds of races—the fickle, Janis-faced vehicles for glory and regret.

The shortest are the sprint races: 1,000 meters for masters, 2,000 meters for college. Geezers don't race against the young bucks except for those few who refuse to acknowledge their over-the-hillness. Masters categories go in approximately five year increments, so at age 68 I was a "G," looking forward to being seventy so I could be, and now am, an "H." One hopes, with no malice intended, that the fast ones have quit or croaked, or are left behind because they are a year or two younger. Masters rowing is the only enterprise I know where people want to fudge their age up; save underage drinking, that is.

Paramount in successful racing is getting to the starting line on time. Fate waits for no man and neither do the refs. If late, the best you can hope for is a yellow card warning, but probably you will see the other boats thrashing down the course, and you can sheepishly paddle back in and hope your reading (of the schedule) improves. Likewise, keeping your mouth shut at the starting line is a good idea.

LEGAL FROLIC AND DETOUR

Misspeaking is hardly new in the history of human foibles, and lately we have had some high officials who routinely butcher the Mother Tongue. But back in the early days of English Common Law, misspeaking could have disastrous results. For example, if a lawyer said: "My client took the chicken" instead of "My client cooked the chicken" his client might be found to be a chicken thief rather than a chicken eater so the lawyer would have to yell "jeofails," referencing the statute that gave the Court authority to amend. High drama, don't you think?

I learned this from Orlando John Hollis's course on Code Pleading. He was Dean of the Oregon Law School for thirty-five years and along with the Honorable Judge Gus Solomon (no kidding, that was really his name) could loosen the bowls of lawyers with a single question.

Apropos of nothing here, the philosophy of law is called jurisprudence. A thorough understanding of jurisprudence will not help you in the least in deciphering the rules of rowing. For example, you can get a yellow card at the FISA World Regatta for having mismatched hats in the boat.

Head races aren't what you might think from the name: a bunch of people piling into a boat and toking. Actually, I was sitting in my car watching my son Aaron's soccer game a number of years ago—sitting in the car because it was raining in Portland—SURPRISE—when the lacrosse players from the next field finished, all got into a couple of cars, and toked up big time. Gamers, they were.

I lost my train of thought here. Head races are so named because they once were run upstream where the current is swifter so the rowers could be more physically challenged, but not go as far. They are typically in the fall and while a sprint race over 1,000 meters is three to four minutes, a head race is seventeen to twenty depending on the length of the race and whether you finish first or last. The other major difference is that sprints are run in seven parallel lanes marked with buoys and head races are one at a time with a running start.

The Port of Toledo, Oregon has a Wooden Boat Festival each summer with an accompanying nine-mile race. I have run it several times, each with its own unique disaster. The falling tide concealed many of the snags so they were predictably hittable the first year. I was rowing Leah's wherry, leaks and all. A sheriff's boat plowed along ahead of the field assuring an ocean type experience, and at the end Leah was there to help and we dropped the truck keys in the water, never to be seen again.

The second year, I put my oars in backwards and as I struggled back to shore a helpful official grabbed hold of my oar and flipped me. Showering before the race—a quaint concept. Aluminum riggers can be straightened but they don't stay straight.

Rowton

Neither do criminals, those recidivist bastards.

The third year, because of those pesky tides, they decided to run the race up the bay from Sawyer's Landing to the Port docks. This isn't a sanctioned race and there are no referees, stake boats, course markers, or, for that matter, rules. So off we went on an uncharted course, and I was ahead waiting for a guy who was about 200 meters behind to fade. He wouldn't. It was like *Butch Cassidy and the Sundance Kid*: "Who is that guy?"

About seven miles in we came to the stretch by the Toledo (not by a long shot, international) airport. I heard some people yelling and knew my friend's house was over there so I—WHAM. Smack into a piling. The boat was damaged, not ruined. I wasn't sure about myself. I was kicking trying to right the boat in the scummy outflow of the sewage treatment plant. Each time I kicked I would hit another piling cut off under the water. (They used to tie up log rafts of the Sometimes a Great Notion variety here.)

Finally, a guy in a row boat let me climb in, and from there get back into my damaged single to limp on. The Butch Cassidy guy had waited, partly out of concern that I not perish and partly because he didn't know where we were supposed to end up. The last two miles were agony. I was hurt and spent and mad and stinky. The organizers encouraged me not to stay for the awards ceremony.

The last year I rowed my Graham Sea Ranger (that's "Sea Ranger," as in "Lone Ranger" in your best radio announcer voice). It is essentially a canoe with riggers and a drop in sliding seat. I thought a big Welch flag on the stern would be a nice touch. Of course I got my ass kicked, losing to a kayak and two guys in a canoe. I also learned to appreciate why rowing seats have a cutout in the front for your tail bone since I left a lot of skin on my shorts.

PHILOSOPHICAL OBSERVATION

I'm not doing that race again no matter how large a role I am playing in my life.

Back to the 1,000-meter "real" races. Usually there are platforms or anchored boats at the start. The referee invites the boats that are queued up to enter the course which means rowing just past the platform and backing in to it so the person lying on her stomach can grab hold of your stern and hold your boat in place. Good luck if there is a cross wind.

An alignment judge, armed with a white flag, instructs various lanes to go in a foot, out three inches until all are even. Then the starter reads the names of the competitors in each lane (while the wind is trying to blow your boat sideways), raises a red flag and says "go" as the flag comes down. (They used to say Etes-vous prets? Partez! which was classier, being French and all. But since not all starters were Frenchly literate, Partez! came out sounding like Party! which confused the rowers since the party was supposed to be after, not before, the race.)

Seasoned racers know that you go when the flag starts down, not when you hear the "go," so you have to watch. In my first singles race I managed, by looking up at the starter, to lift my oars out of the water so that my first two strokes were in the air—clean wiffs. The young lady holding my boat had a perplexed look saying with her eyes: "why are you still here?"

Most starts are ¼ stroke, ½, ¾, lengthen, full and then twenty hard fast strokes to try to get the lead before settling into a sustainable pace for the body of the race. The thrashing and exhortations of half a dozen coxswains in the first 100 meters of a race is thrilling and a race between evenly matched boats in adjacent lanes, sublime.

Pain. The reason mental toughness is an essential part of racing is that rowers know the pain will come and enduring it, gritting through it, is part of the deal. The sprint at the start of the race is to get ahead of the other boats so that you can see them and they can't see you. Your boat can then react if they begin to close, and they, knowing you are out of sight, may get discouraged.

But the sprint at the beginning still leaves three-quarters of the race to go, and the lactic acid that is the byproduct of muscles eating themselves up from the anaerobic start, results in PAIN. The highest levels of lactic acid found in the blood streams of athletes—about thirty parts per million—were in rowers.

Philosophical Digression

If you ask a winning rower to describe a race, most can't tell you much. The condition is called "flow." There is a book by that name that I would put in a footnote if I hadn't said I wouldn't—the author is Mihaly Csikszentmihalyi. Read it. Flow is that out of body condition where you are so attuned to what you are doing as to lose all sense of time and place. Rowers call it "swing." Trial lawyers who have destroyed a witness on cross-examination can't remember what they asked (this rarely happens no matter what they tell you). Concert pianists remember only that the concerto started and ended. We are venturing dangerously close to the field of metaphysics here, but to demythologize, when you hear metaphysics just think "abstract" and fergedaboutit.

More Philosophy Than You Want to Know

Actually, *Flow* is a lot like Immanuel Kant's *ding an sich*. If you walk into a barbershop and ask the guys there if they have figured out the *ding an sich* they will think you are telling a sex joke. It means "the thing in itself" and refers to that whose existence is certain but whose essence is unknowable.

Rowton

Like God, maybe, except God's existence isn't certain unless one is a believer and believers don't need no ding an sich.

Kant didn't have any of my writing teachers who would have rapped his knuckles with a ruler for using the word "thing" in the first place. But since it remains unknowable, I suppose thing is as good a word for it as any. More on that later.

One More Race

There is a wonderful race called the Head of the Gorge on Vancouver Island, B.C. (That makes it sound like it is on land—it is actually overseen by the stately and elegant Empress Hotel in Victoria Harbor.) Since it is in the late fall, the second and third most serious concerns are not freezing to death waiting to start, and not getting landed upon by a seaplane. The first most serious concern is getting to the starting line because you have to row through the gorge which is tidal and narrow and has big rocks on either side.

Philosophical (Greek, Anyway) Comment

In Homeric legend, sailors, who are by definition horny, were lured by the sirens (babes) as they tried to navigate around the rocks and avoid being eaten by Scylla, a six headed monster, or perishing in the whirlpool of Charybdis.

The Head of the Gorge doesn't have sirens, but it does have an "angel" sitting on the rocks with a megaphone, and by god you better listen when he says: "Bow and seven seats row hard, NOW." You get two tries to make it through and then you have to go to the back of the line and probably will miss your start. There are hundreds of spectators on the rocks and the bridge above because watching to see if any boats end up on the rocks is more fun than watching a race any day. It's called Schadenfreude.

After races, the winners get medals. My favorite presentation is at the Worlds where the winning boat in each flight paddles from the finish line to the grandstand dock and officials drape a medal around each rower's neck. I have only watched this. Bugger.

CHAPTER 12

Desiderius Erasmus (1466–1536)

"I hate one that remembers what's done over the cup." Erasmus

He named himself and you may never have heard of him, but some think him the most influential scholar of all time. (We have advanced about 1,000 years after Augustine here, but during the Dark Ages, rowing and philosophy both gave way to baser pursuits.) Desiderius and Erasmus mean desired in Latin and Greek respectively. His parents called him Gerrit Gerritzoon and hereafter I will call him what the whole of the educated world of his time called him: Erasmus. He was born in Rotterdam in 1466, received a religious education, and became a wandering scholar. What really made his reputation was his publication, around the year 1500, of a book called *The Adages*. It originally contained 800 sayings and proverbs, many from the Bible, and many that are familiar to us today: "he is fighting his own shadow," "to chomp at the bit," "leave no stone unturned," "where there is smoke there is fire."

The Adages was later expanded to include more than 3,000 sayings and became the second most popular book in Europe (after the Bible) at a time when Guttenberg's printing press was making books a reachable possession to more than the 5 percent of the population that was educated. In fact, Erasmus was a great champion of widespread education and was a teacher of teachers.

Erasmus loved Plato but not Aristotle. He thought man was created in the image of God, but that the Aristotelian system, as expanded by Augustine, that had been the glue holding society together during the Middle Ages, got in the way of man's relationship to God. He remained a priest all of his life, and even argued with Martin Luther over the issue of man's free will, but he was tremendously influential in promoting the kind of thinking that fueled the Reformation. He was a modern thinker, full of wit and charm and irreverence.

Erasmus believed the church had distorted the simple teachings of Jesus. He despised intolerance, persecution, and dishonest thinking. He taught that a person's chief duties are to be charitable, open minded, and intelligent, and he was not shy in pointing out the foibles of his fellow humans. In fact, he wrote a whole book about foibles and pretentions entitled *In Praise of Folly*.

Folly is dedicated to Thomas More, later to be St. Thomas More, after Henry VIII whacked off his head. He wrote *Folly* while living at More's house in London. Erasmus was a constant correspondent and friend with the thinkers of the age in England, Italy, the low countries, France and Germany. Folly, herself, is the narrator who exposes the foolishness, self-delusion, and stupidity of classes of people, and few escape Erasmus' acerbic wit and keen eye. Lying orators and poets, church officials, those who claim wisdom (and whose beards are common only with goats) get reamed. Philosophers, in particular, take a beating. "Their continual and restless thoughts insensibly prey upon their spirits and dry up their radical moisture." Don't let that happen to you. Paradoxically, Folly says that it is folly itself that keeps one young. The point here is that being human is being stupid, at least some of the time.

In Praise of Folly includes observations on husbands and wives, soldiers and commanders, the scholar and his tutor, the governor and the governed and looking back over the space of 500 years, these human shortcomings are absolutely and firmly implanted in our own behavior as if the book had been written yesterday. Wisdom, or what passes for it, is a true obstacle to getting things done. Pretense, blathering and preening fit the human being like a suit of clothes, and Erasmus takes great pleasure in holding up the mirror to our shortcomings and inflated egos. Including himself. He ends by having Folly say: "Sometimes a fool may speak a word in season." But don't expect me, he says, to remember a word I said.

In his voluminous correspondence with the great thinkers of Europe, and through his books and papers, Erasmus became the leading figure in forming humanistic thought for the turbulent 16th century and, arguably, he had as much to do with the course of the Reformation as did Martin Luther.

It is difficult to read Erasmus and then today's news reportage of the preening and strutting of Congress and not conclude that folly is the very definition of humans both then and now.

CHAPTER 13

Rowing as Healing

> "Accept the challenges so that you may feel the exhilaration of victory."
> Fortune cookie message

Life deals some nasty cards, even to the strongest, the smartest, and the fittest. No one deserves ill fortune—well, perhaps there are a few who have earned it, but in my experience, life doesn't work that way. I don't see the universe as being controlled by the hand of God, or the Devil, or the Great Pumpkin.

Years ago I represented some particularly pious clients involved in a contentious trial. Trials are rollercoaster events. Good days and bad; exhilaration and despair. When things were going well, "God had His hand in it"; when they weren't, they prayed without interval. Did it do any good? We lost. Perhaps the unseen hand thought they needed a dose of humility. Perhaps there was an unknowable lesson. Perhaps the hand was flipping them the bird. I certainly don't know. What I do know is that we had bad facts, the law was against us and we lost because we lost.

On the macro scale, mortals can't do much about earthquakes, famine or even the constant scourge of war. On the micro—the personal—scale, we can be positive, eat right, exercise, and go to bed early and we still might get cancer, heart disease or multiple sclerosis. What to do? Most, I suspect, go through the stages: denial, anger, bargaining, reconciliation, and then what?

Row, that's what. My friend who is a great coach, a great leader of rowers and an all-around great person has, herself, endured a lifetime of medical challenges. She maintains an unflappable, if a bit acerbic, optimism. I asked where she had been and she responded, "fighting mortality." When I called her, she had just gotten out of the hospital and was a little goofy from whatever medications she had taken. She told me to remind her of this conversation on Friday, if she didn't remember. On Friday she was back in the hospital.

What she said is that coaching a crew of breast cancer survivors had made her a better coach. These women are so motivated that her job is to keep them from overtraining and hurting themselves. Each one of them is committed to life, to being strong, to getting better. They row to exhaustion. They go to bed at 8 p.m. and dream of rowing. It can be an addiction, she says and not all addictions are bad. (I would quibble with the word addiction. An addiction controls you and I would like to think that in a sport you control your part in it no matter how compelling it is.)

But Rowology is not the toll-free road to salvation. Another friend, a strong and dedicated rower, has been on both chemotherapy and radiation, has lost her hair and suffered multiple indignities and still doesn't have a definitive diagnosis, let alone a prognosis. She says, "I will be the fittest patient ever." After her first, after her second, after her third round of chemotherapy she waited for the bad stuff—the barfing, the fever, the achiness, the hurties. None of that visited her at all. Was it because she is so fit? Medical science probably couldn't prove it, but I am going to say yes. Rowology, however, doesn't have a salvation tab. Rowing may help your health, but it won't, by itself, make you well.

Paradoxically, though, it does heal. So much of being well resides in attitude—in deciding what you can control and what you can't and concentrating on the former. Here is an example as written by the great American author, Wallace Stegner. His subject was John Wesley Powell who explored much of the American Southwest, was an early conservationist and the first Director of Public Lands for the Country. Major Powell lost an arm in the Civil War battle of Shiloh. Stegner writes: "Losing one's right arm is a misfortune; to some it would be a disaster, to others an excuse. It affected Wes Powell about as much as a stone fallen into a swift stream affects the course of the river. With a velocity like his, he simply foamed over it." Indeed he did, organizing the first party successfully to float the Grand Canyon, climbing sheer cliffs to take geological readings—he booked no suggestion that his body was less than whole.

Every major regatta now has races for handicapped rowers. Handicapped is an inadequate word because it derives from "handy with the cap"—a beggar. These rowers are anything but. They are cheerful, determined, admirable and tough, proving that experience is not what happens to you, but what you do with what happens to you.

ROWTON

Easy for you to say.

Good point. Were I a believer, I would say I have been blessed: with health, with love, with enough brains to struggle, with quality parents who brought me up in a land of plenty. And believer or not, I am grateful. The anvil may drop on my head any day, or I may get a pass. No way of knowing. But that is all the more reason to "make hay while the sun shines" (one of the aphorisms of Erasmus).

We have slipped seamlessly into ethics here. Ethics guides us in thinking about how we might handle the kind of sinkers life pitches before they reach the plate. Ethics is about anticipation. Ethics is having a plan for a game where the rules, the boundaries and the competitors are fluid, unknown and devious. That is why ethics—useable ethics—doesn't consist of rules, but rather kinds of reactions. Ethics is not ironclad rules of right and wrong, not pious declarations but actions in the most existential sense. It is not what we think or say but what we do. The ethics judge is the one in the mirror. The ethical conclusion is how you feel about what you did or didn't do. It is a gyro, not a compass.

Where does how you feel come from? Freud said we have an alter ego that speaks to us (like that damnable Rowton). Plato said there is a natural law that is knowable to those that seek it. Our society makes demands on us, as do our families, friends and even enemies. There are rules of war that govern behavior in the least civilized situations. One of my many quarrels with Christianity is the notion that if you sin in your heart, you just plain sin. Cut us some slack. Leave us the fantasy, I say. One could argue, and I do, that the fantasy is a release that prevents sexual assault, defuses anger, even retards war. What happens in our heads is ours. Whether we are pure of heart means a whole lot less than whether our actions benefit humankind.

Rowton

OK smart guy, you've jettisoned the god head but the Judeo-Christian morality so infuses western culture that yours is a distinction without a difference. It just leaves you free to cherry pick those parts you like and leave out the rest. I say morality without context is like jello without a bowl.

My point is not to have a system at all. The goal is not moral certainty, but rather to be ethically constant, ethically aware, and ethically meticulous. Ambiguity is the nature of the world, and few of us will be able to say, in retrospect, that we acted absolutely correctly because when ethical issues arise, the choices are almost always tainted. Sometimes all of them are bad. Moral confidence comes from having decided how we want to live our lives and what values we cherish. We will make mistakes, we will feel guilty, we will be sorry. Those are all normal and healthy. Our resolve to do better, to keep trying, to think about our past decisions shows we have an ethical pulse.

You might have noticed, certainly the Rowton did, that I have used morals and ethics interchangeably here. The dictionary will say that ethics is standards of conduct and morals, determinations of right and wrong. I just don't find those definitions, or the distinction between the two very helpful in the real world.

How do we build ethical muscle? Same way we build physical muscle: practice and repetition. Read as many philosophers as you can and take from each what is meaningful to you. Then keep the books and read them again in a few years and take what appeals to you then and keep doing it for the rest of your life. Think about ethical issues and talk about them and consider the issues that arise daily in the news. Repetition has a profound place in living our lives. There is, of course the rowing stroke, but think also of the repetition in Beethoven's 4th Symphony or the instrumental solo in the middle of *Baby Let Me Light Your Fire* by the Doors or the refrain of any gospel song or Phillip Glass' Piano Etude #2. Repetition turns something on in our brains that helps us be ethically prepared.

Back to rowing as healing. Depression is a scourge. It sucks the life out of the best of us. There are drugs that help, but for those I have talked to who have it, the best treatment is regular, vigorous exercise that gets those endorphins dancing on their toes. That is an instance where rowing really does heal. Theodore Roosevelt put it this way: "Black care rarely sits behind a rider whose pace is fast enough."

CHAPTER 14

Descartes (1596–1650)

"What the river says, that is what I say." William Stafford, poet

Descartes (pronounced *day-cart*) put his mathematical gifts to work by becoming a card sharp at age eighteen, calculating and beating the odds at the Paris tables. One of history's true geniuses, he changed the direction of philosophy from God revealed to reason deduced, thus allowing persons of either gender and any walk of life to use intellect to guide their lives. It was a big enough deal to accord him the singular honor of having all of his published works placed on the **Index of Prohibited Books** by Pope Alexander VII in 1663. By that time Descartes didn't care, having been dead for thirteen years, but during his lifetime, he was constantly on the run, moving first to Protestant Holland where he lived in a different place almost every year, and thence to Scandinavia where he continued to perch rather than dwell.

Rowton

Just because your author here doesn't mention any philosophers between St. Augustine in the fifth century and Descartes, twelve centuries later (except for Erasmus) doesn't mean there weren't any. Lots of fun stuff went on, especially in the High Middle Ages. It was closely tied to religion and dictated the social order in the West. Eastern philosophy was arguably way ahead of the rest of the globe but your writer here doesn't know beans about it. If you are interested, ditch this book and have at it.

Here, to assuage the Rowton, is a tidbit. In the early twelfth century, Hugh of St. Victor said that all knowledge from whatever source is essential on the road to wisdom. He wrote in *Didascalicon* that philosophy consists of four master categories: theoretical, practical, mechanical, and logical. By the theoretical, we identify truth, by the practical, virtue, and by the mechanical, we get "relief of physical existence." The logical category ties it all together by allowing us to see how the first three are interconnected. But here is the thing for rowers: Hugh's mechanical celebrated the practical and physical such as agriculture, hunting, theatre, and by inescapable logic, rowing. So there you have it—put those monks in a boat and they think great thoughts.

Before the Rowton distracted me, I was discussing Descartes. Through methodological skepticism Descartes reduced what he knew to one indisputable precept: thought exists. Because thought exists, and I think, I know I exist. Bingo. The single best known phrase in philosophy: *cogito ergo sum*—I think, therefore I am.

Our senses are unreliable so the only true source of knowledge is from reason. His emphasis on theoretical mathematics, on the link between math and physics, and on the properties of light was prologue to the work of Newton and Einstein. And while a long standing philosophical debate has raged over the centuries between empiricists such as Hume and Cartesians (from the Latin form of Descartes' name, Cartesius), Descartes did appreciate the need for experimentation as a way to verify pure thought. In fact he embarked on a search to determine where the soul resided in the body. He did this by cutting up corpses in the Paris morgue—an undertaking (no pun intended) not typical for philosophers. He determined that the pineal gland housed the soul, but of course, it left the premises when the host expired.

Rowing owes a debt to Descartes. He developed analytic geometry, creating the commonly known symbols x, y, and z for unknowns and a, b, and c for knowns and then using algebra to describe geometry. He discovered an early form of the law of conservation of mechanical momentum, $P=mv$: the momentum of a boat equals the mass times the velocity. The heavier the boat, the more work it takes to get it up to speed. That is why rowing is such a demanding sport. The hardest work is at the start of the race to get the vessel moving, and after expending all of the energy, the rowers can't just coast, they have to keep it moving for the next 1,900 meters.

Galileo, when challenged by the Inquisition, recanted his writings (the Church *knew* the sun revolved around the earth) and Descartes lived his life as witness to the slaughter of Catholics and Protestants by each other during the seventeenth century. As a matter of personal preservation, Descartes spent a lifetime arguing that scientific projects confirmed, indeed proved, the existence of God, which was, he said, "at least as certain as any geometrical proof." And while Descartes argued that God could not deceive him, his legacy is to have set the mind free to go where it will.

Rowton

Descartes chickened out in the God department. But it was more than just self preservation. Monotheism, and especially disputes between believers in the same God have perpetrated many of the world's great slaughters. He saw that first hand but still was unwilling to acknowledge that if there were a God, He had fomented calamity by those who purport to serve Him.

The Rowton talks like he learned to speak in a machine shop.

CHAPTER 15

The Workout

"The winds and the waves are on the side of the ablest navigators."
Edward Gibbon

The splendid and satisfying moment is hearing the horn toot as you cross the finish line ahead of all others. But such success is conceived in the quiet determination with which we challenge every day, every practice, every physical and mental barrier. Champions are made in the erg barn, running stadium steps, rowing in the rain and the chop. Just flailing away will not do. The workout must be according to a plan—a plan to which we adhere slavishly. Celebrated rowing coach Harry Parker put it this way: "There are two seats in rowing. One is in the boat and the other is on the shore. You choose."

NECESSARY DIGRESSION

Like right now I am tempted to go down and see what's in the fridge even though I just sat down to write five minutes ago. I know a writer who literally chained herself to her desk to keep from being distracted by almost everything. As the famous opera singer Beverly Sills observed: "You may be disappointed if you fail, but you are doomed if you don't try."

What kind of a plan? Depends on your goal. If keeping in shape, yukking it up with your pals and getting fresh air is what you seek (and I by no means discredit your goal), then just getting in and rowing three or four times a week will probably do it and you will have a lot of fun. If on the other hand, you want constantly to improve as a rower, to race and win, to maximize your potential, then things get a lot more serious and require a degree of commitment akin to joining the army.

Mike Caviston, the University of Michigan Women's rowing coach, devised the "Wolverine Plan." Fortunately for him, that is the name of his team; otherwise he would be in a world of trouble. He posted the plan on the web and a lot of clubs and schools use it.

The purpose of the plan is to maximize performance, and to do that it requires adherence to a specific training schedule with principles, parameters, and benchmarks, just like physics or chemistry or chess. The overload principle is that the athlete must challenge herself physiologically to adapt (grow). This means lots of practices of long duration and varied intensity.

A second concept is the specificity principle meaning the athlete must perform the bulk of training actually doing the sport—rowing. The reversibility principle is the nastiest. It holds that gains are not permanent and if you stop training, they go away. I would add another corollary, and that is that it takes months to make a gain and days to lose it.

The final governing principle is individual differences—that we are put together differently and come into training at different levels and with different tolerances so that a single, microwave-able product will not work. The idea is to maximize the chances for expanding personal potential.

Philosophical Interlude

Before we get to the nuts and bolts of the Wolverine Plan—a physical training system—we should acknowledge that intellectual systems are the mother's milk, the beluga caviar, the bee's knees of philosophy and particularly theology (the philosophy of religion). Paul Tillich did theology in his native language, German, until in about 1933 when he fled Hitler and came to Union Theological Seminary in the United States. Later he remarked that when he switched to writing in English, not only did the language change, but the theology did, too. Language does that to us. For example, if you address someone in German, the form of the language tells if that person is male or female, young or old. If I write "you" in English, I could be talking about anybody. (I am, however, talking to *you*, *Liebchen*.) "The limits of my language are the limits of my world" said Austrian philosopher Ludwig Wittgenstein.

One of my colleagues at the University of Chicago was writing his doctoral thesis on Tillich who at that point had published two of the promised three volumes of his *Systematic Theology*. My friend's project was to predict what Tillich would write in his third volume, and when it came out posthumously, my friend wasn't just a little wrong, he was spectacularly wrong in every particular. They still call him "Professor."

Back to Mike Caviston's Wolverine Plan. Training is in four levels, level 1 being as hard as you can go for short intervals with ample recovery time (active recovery means you keep rowing, but at a relaxed pace and pressure to minimize fatigue, increase circulation and promote removal of metabolic waste products like lactic acid). Level 2 is the hardest because you are going at about 95 percent but for longer intervals. Level 3 focuses on endurance with long duration and 85 percent power and level 4 makes up the majority of training with long intervals at 65–70 percent capacity.

The plan is complicated, requires charting of each day's performance, demands complete buy in by the rower, and mixes the levels from practice to practice. This description doesn't do it justice, but here is what Mike would tell you about it: "Before you complain about what a crock the Wolverine Plan is, take time to read the damn thing. Read it all. Read it three or four times if you have to. If you don't have the discipline to READ it, you don't have the discipline to USE it."

SUCCESS WITHOUT A PLAN

David Challinor was seventy-five when I rowed with him at the Potomac Boat Club and he would jump into the stroke seat of a double scull and take off. I was thirty years younger and I would come home stepping on my tongue. David liked to row up the wrong side of the river. He said the trick was to row where the rocks weren't. That was fine. But I was in the bow and supposedly in charge of steering and it was all I could do to keep up with this madman who, while he was killing me, carried on a botanical lecture about how some trees along the bank emitted a kind of poison that kept other plants away. Maybe David had a plan; mine was to survive.

MORE TILLICH

Comparing Challinor's success (he was the guy to beat at the Head of the Charles for years) and Caviston's Wolverine Plan (his team has excelled at the NCAAs) just goes to show that Tillich was right: "The awareness of the ambiguity of one's highest achievements as well as one's deepest failures is a definite sign of moral maturity."

ROWTON

Ambiguity is the all-purpose rag of philosophical discourse, particularly if you don't understand what the hell is going on.

CHAPTER 16

Jeremy Bentham (1748–1832) and John Stuart Mill (1806–1873)

"Don't Worry, Be Happy." Bobby McFerrin

Bobby McFerrin's song "Don't Worry, Be Happy" has, at this writing, received more than fourteen million hits on YouTube. That should tell us something about the universality of the pursuit of happiness. There even is a philosophical term for it: hedonics. Hedonics is the study of what makes experience in life pleasant or unpleasant. It embraces the whole range of human circumstances from the biological to the societal.

ROWTON

Hedonics is one field in which students are more than happy, thrilled even, to do field work.

Being happy is harder than it would seem. In fact, most of us humans do a pretty good job of screwing up our lives, and that is why both philosophy and religion spend a lot of mental and emotional wattage trying to create a game plan whereby happiness can be real.

Perhaps the simplest iteration comes from the Gospel of John: "This I command you, to love one another." The logic is equally straight forward: "God the Father loves you and therefore, you should love each other." But as two millennia of history show us, commanding someone to love, or to be happy, might instill the right intention, but often such love is promoted with swords and bullets.

Is happiness, whether commanded or just sought, totally illusive? It surely is slippery. Japan, from 1958 to 1986, enjoyed a fourfold increase in per capita income without any reported increase in personal satisfaction. To the contrary, increased economic prosperity often breeds increased alcoholism, depression, suicide, drug use, and anxiety.

In the year 1900 the typical American family lived in a dwelling about the size of today's garage. They didn't have electricity, cars, or indoor plumbing, but they did have a lot of togetherness as families, often including several generations under the same roof. Community is one of the ingredients for more happiness than we enjoy today. We are wired, as mammals, to live in community. An isolated monkey will repeatedly pull a lever giving a glimpse of another monkey, with no other reward.

And so we row. Together. To be happy. In the rain.

ROWTON

Hemmingway my ass.

Access to nature is another happiness generator that is hardwired in our DNA. All humans came from the African savanna, and not all that long ago in geological time. As city dwellers and electronic screen addicts, our lifestyles isolate us from nature and that isolation negatively affects our happiness.

That's why we row. To be outside. And to win. Winning, by the way, is defined as success, not necessarily coming in first. First means getting the medals, but success may mean beating one's personal best or even just finishing the race. All of those can feel good.

Some rowing venues are more natural than others, but even the most urban has water. (During the floods of a few years ago the Oregon State men's crew was rowing pairs on the golf course. None of the skeggs—fins on the bottom of the boats—survived). Most water has herons and beavers and nutria and fish and trees and rocks and wind and even sometimes snow. In short, the natural world is good for our health. That is why we hike and hunt and camp and take flowers to the sick.

I don't mean to suggest that money is not important to happiness, but all of the studies I have seen show that the floor is about $10,000 per capita per year. That is $40,000 for a family of four and even in the United States, the richest country in history, many of our citizens fall below that level. Above a certain level, all of the statistics tell us that more money will not make you happier.

BENTHAM AND MILL, FINALLY

Jeremy Bentham, who died in 1832, followed David Hume as a champion of empirical observation. The title of his book, *An Introduction to the Principles of Morals and Legislation*, sounds like one of the great oxymorons of all time. Since when did morals have anything to do with legislation? He thought they did. Moreover, he thought one could put a precise scientific value on pleasure and pain and that the function of the social order should be to maximize pleasure and minimize pain.

He called this social hedonism. He did not mean unchecked licentiousness, but rather an ordered society that would produce the greatest happiness for the greatest number. Indeed, he bleached the raunchiness out of human interactions by his sevenfold mathematical index for pleasure which measured **intensity**—how powerful is the pleasure; **duration**—how long lasting; **certainty**—is it guaranteed?; **proximity**—how close is the pleasure?; **fecundity**—will this activity generate additional pleasures?; **purity**—how pain-free is this pleasure?; and **extent**—how many other citizens will experience it? I know, you are probably wondering how an orgy would measure up, but he called this formula "The Calculus of Felicity" and from that you can conclude that an orgy was the last thing on his mind. Lover of life that he was, Bentham left his mummified remains to be present at every trustee's meeting of University College, London. He sits there stuffed but inert to this day. His philosophy goes by the sexless name, utilitarianism.

John Stuart Mill, who died in 1873, went beyond Bentham in emphasizing the quality of pleasure and not just the quantity. It is better to be a dissatisfied human than a satisfied pig. Don't ask how he knew this. He also followed the Platonic mind body distinction by classifying higher pleasures as those of the intellect and lower pleasures as those of the body.

Mill's *On Liberty*, 1859, argues that one can interfere with another's liberty only for self-protection. He wrote:

"The only purpose for which power can be rightfully exercised over any member of a civilized community against his will is to prevent harm to others. His own good, either physical or moral, is not sufficient warrant. He cannot rightfully be compelled to do or to forebear…because in the opinion of others to do so would be wise or even right."

Particularly as to free speech, he said that society is harmed by suppression of ideas—even wrong-headed ideas. What seems like a false idea may be proved to be true, and without dissent, true opinion becomes "dead dogma." His wit had sharp edges: "conservatives are not necessarily stupid, but most stupid people are conservative."

As to limitations on speech, he used the example that one cannot falsely yell "fire" in a crowded theatre, a construct still used in United States First Amendment law. There is a difference between a newspaper publishing an opinion that corn sellers starve the poor (which is allowed) and the same opinion being shouted to an angry mob before a corn seller's house (disallowed). This is the concept of clear and present danger used, for example, in the Supreme Court's decision in *Brandenburg v. Ohio*, 395 U.S. 444 (1969).

Mill's other famous book is *The Subjugation of Women* in which he called for equal rights. He was a champion of liberty of conscience, of thought, of religion, of association, and of doing what we like with our lives. He argued that censorship, intolerance, and imposed conformity are some of the greatest dangers facing society. While many of Mill's precepts were embraced by our Bill of Rights (the first ten amendments to the Constitution), you decide how much progress we have made on these issues in the last 200 years.

ALFRED E. NEUMAN AND BHUTAN

I grew up with Mad Comic Books and Mad grew up, in so far as it ever did, with Alfred E. Neuman, a gap-toothed, loppy eared purveyor of the slogan: "what, me worry?" His face appeared on a lot of different bodies including those of Darth Vader, President George W. Bush, Santa, and Bart Simpson. He ran as a write in candidate for president in 1956 under the slogan: "You could do worse…and always have." The profound among the frivolous here is that humor is one of the great secrets of being happy. If we can laugh, both at ourselves, and with others, we can be well both physiologically and mentally. So here are some of Alfred E. Neuman's pronouncements:

> If opera is entertainment then falling off a roof is transportation.
>
> Most people are so lazy that they cannot even exercise good judgment.
>
> How come stealing from one book is plagiarism, but stealing from many is research?
>
> The United Nations is a place where governments that oppose free speech demand to be heard.

The small country of Bhutan, in the foothills of the Himalayan Mountains, has taken happiness seriously enough to have a measurable Gross National Happiness (GNH) quotient. In 1972 the Fourth Dragon King initiated a sophisticated four- to five-hour survey that measured the well-being of each citizen, utilizing Buddhist theology and based on the four pillars of sustainable development, preservation of cultural values, conservation of the natural environment, and establishment of good government.

ROWTON

And we call what we have in the West, "civilization."

Economic development must pass a GNH impact review much like the Environmental Impact Statements required in the United States. Among the issues decided was whether to have television, how to control visitors, and how to give access to remote villages without ruining their splendid isolation. The society is highly animistic. Moving a rock may offend the spirit of that rock, so a whole raft of considerations are in play, and not just "can I make money here?" That and their famous archery competitions make Bhutan a lovely and happy place, but what really makes Bhutan unique is that its society is formed around social and psychological considerations more than economics.

Chapter 17

Gear

>Lawyer: "And what gear were you in at the time of the accident?"
>Witness: "I had on Gucci sweats and Reeboks."

It will cost you well over $1,000 to get into ski gear—skies, boots, and poles—and that is before the helmet, pants, parka, goggles, gloves, four wheel drive Porsche, etc. For rowing all you need is a pair of lycra shorts and a tee shirt (assuming a club provides the boat and oars). The reason for tight shorts is that you want them to be long enough to protect the underside of your thigh from the seat, but not baggy enough that the bottom of the pant leg gets caught between the track and the wheels as the seat moves back and forth.

You are way too busy during practices to worry about your clothes looking good. Anyway, they are going to get pretty sweaty, and as you peel off layers during the practice those clothes end up in the bottom of the boat where the water sloshes around. There is water in the bottom of the boat because coaches take great pleasure in "waking" the shells: driving the launch alongside to create a huge swell that hits broadside and fills up the boat. And the oars splash when they go into the water. I'm with Thoreau who cautioned us to distrust any enterprise that requires new clothes.

Our coach says there is no such thing as cold weather; only bad clothes. So when there is ice on the dock and ramp, a few extra precautions are required because we are going out, that is clear. To get the ice off the ramp, which when the river is down, can be quite steep, we slosh buckets of river water on it (and necessarily on ourselves, too). This, however, is a very bad idea if the temperature is still below freezing, so the alternative fix is to lay down blankets or towels.

Philosophical Fallacy

Our icy ramp is the real slippery slope. The metaphysical slippery slope, sometimes also known as the camel's nose in the tent, the thin edge of the wedge, the don't give an inch, the crack in the foundation, or during the Vietnam War, the domino theory is the argument that if a single exception to a rule is made, the whole house of cards will collapse, always with disastrous results. The argument is logical hogwash, but it is durable.

The latest example I encountered was in a conversation with an adjacent land owner. I had called him because some folks were blasting away with shotguns at the geese that use his pond. Not unlike the geese I too wanted to use the pond since it is a perfect half mile winter rowing venue only 200 yards outside my front door. No, he said, if he let me use it, everybody else would want to row there. Yeah, sure, all the other rowers who live in this farming community of which there are exactly none. I suppose I could just use it like the geese do, but then again, I could get shot.

Back to winter, clothes and the rowers that love it. If icy, we carry down the eights with a dozen people rather than the usual eight so that we look like a white shelled centipede crawling down to the dock. And finally we try not to fall in (unlike a teammate who shall remain unnamed, who missed a step between the ramp and the dock and disappeared without a trace. It was nice to know you, Tom).

Poagies are fleece devices that slip over the oar handle so you can grip the oar and still have something to keep the backs of your hands warm. Gloves are for wussies, and it is hard to grip the oar properly with them on.

That reminds me that I have yet to tell you about feathering and blade work, arguably the most important part of the stroke. Feathering means rolling the oar blade so it is horizontal to the water on the recovery, and then gradually rolling it back so that at the precise moment it drops into the water, it is exactly perpendicular. With a sweep oar, feathering is done with the inside hand, while the outside hand taps the oar out of the water and after the catch, transfers the power of the legs to the oar during the drive. For sculling oars, you feather both at the same time by rolling your wrists.

At the catch (when the oar drops in) there should be a little back splash which shows that the oar has gone in at the precise moment the rower reaches the top of the slide and the slide reverses direction for the power part of the stroke. As the oar comes out of the water at the release there should be very little splash, but instead, a vicious whirlpool of water your blade has moved. The oar shaft actually flexes during the power stroke, and the more cavitation, the faster you go. The blade creates a hole in the water that makes it easier to pop it out at the end of the stroke. Twisting the torso toward the oar at the top of the slide allows the rower to get more length on each stroke.

Philosophical Reflection

Philosophy tends to favor linear thinking. Thesis, antithesis, resolution. For example, all cows are warm blooded. I am warm blooded. Therefore, I am a cow. Logic is a big part of philosophy, and since the whole discipline is based on reason and reason builds from facts, philosophers have little patience for sloppy thinking.

Rowton

Ha. Members of the George W. Bush administration claimed they could create their own reality and scoffed at the "fact based community."

Racing uniforms are the only other bit of gear that warrants mention, and again, uniforms are usually modest, consisting of matching shirts and shorts. Some teams wear something called a unisuit which is shorts and a singlet all in one piece. I know of no human being who looks good in a unisuit.

Traditionally, college crews race for shirts, the winner getting the losers sweaty shirts. Why they would want them is another question entirely. And then there are the rowers who graduated from Harvard in 1958 and still wear their shirt that once was crimson in today's race.

Rowton

Superstition has its place, but I chalk it up to poverty.

CHAPTER 18

Immanuel Kant (1724–1804) and William Blake (1757–1827)

"Avoid those with I.Q.s below room temperature." Anon.

Don't start your study of philosophy with Kant. He is worth the effort, but the kind of mental gymnastics required means you have to be in shape, mentally, before you tackle this brainy little dude. He is, after all, the slinger of the *ding an sich* that has a ponder quotient of 99.5 percent.

You would not have found Kant out in a boat. He preferred the "gentle but sensitive tranquility" of the philosopher to the "rapturous flights dreamed of by the mystics." So much a creature of quiet habit was he that the town's folk set their watches by his afternoon stroll. He was a man of the mind alone and was not swayed by strong feelings or unruly impulses. So no power 10s and no thrill of victory—just pure, and sometimes unintelligible, philosophy. An added impediment to pursuing Kant is that his writing style was labeled by contemporary Heinrich Heine as "the grey, dry style of a paper bag." Kant himself described it as "pettifogging and arid." What fun. But buck up; *The Critique of Pure Reason* is only 800 pages long.

At the risk of seeming reductionist in a work on Rowology that cares more about a quick catch (when the blade enters the water, remember?) than the minutia of philosophical theory, Kant cared about two realities: the limits of pure reason, and the autonomy of the soul, that is, free will. Reason, he said, is limited to experience, and therefore is unable to deal with the purely metaphysical questions such as whether our soul is immortal or whether God exists. We gather information through our senses and use our minds to make sense of this information. Understanding (reason) helps us by creating categories and structures that order information.

ROWTON

Reason and observation. Observation and reason. Revelation and authority. Authority and revelation. I think we are caught in an infinite loop.

Metaphysics, on the other hand, is thought that is independent of all experience. He calls this *a priori* knowledge, which is something of a misnomer, since if we can't perceive it by our senses, we can't know it. This is where intuition comes in, giving humans a glimpse that something lies beyond pure reason, but leaving us without the tools to verify or describe it. He wrote: "Metaphysics is a dark ocean without shores or lighthouse strewn with many a philosophical wreck."

Our minds may "transcend" to deal with the noumena (the metaphysical things we cannot see) but we are limited by the phenomena—that which our senses report. That which is beyond our senses is the ding an sich, which may or may not be the same thing as the noumena, but in any case is a reality. His point is that there is more to the world than our senses can handle, but we have no way of knowing what it is. So the phrase "transcendental knowledge" is a total oxymoron: knowledge that cannot be verified.

That brings us to Kant's foundational belief that we have free will. Free will is a metaphysical presumption that underlies his whole system of morality, and as such, it is a house built on sand because the true essence is unknowable—that damn *ding an sich*. It is reminiscent of that scene from the movie *A Few Good Men* where lawyer Tom Cruise yells, "I want the truth," and Jack Nicholson yells back: "You can't handle the truth." The truth, as far as Kant's morality goes, is the categorical imperative: do unto others as you would have them do to you. It is the golden rule that exists in practical every ethical system ever created.

It may seem that Kant is famous just for being obscure. He is, however, regarded as the greatest philosopher of his age, and perhaps of any age. In other words, take the time to dig in and see what you find. One parting shot is the way Kant justifies religion. He says it would not be possible to accept religion if we could rationally know God through observation of the world of phenomena because then we could use our reason to prove religion false. But since we cannot know the nature of God, such faith fits perfectly well with the world that we can see and reason in. This is one big philosophical slight of hand: we set limits on knowledge to make room for religion.

ROWTON

What is it with these high powered thinkers? First Descartes and now Kant don't want anything to do with God and yet they feel compelled to justify His existence. Go figure.

WILLIAM BLAKE

I pair Kant and Blake not just because they were contemporaries, but because their search for knowledge was intense in such different ways. Blake was a quiet, unassuming intellectual bomb thrower. He is lauded by many as one of the finest minds ever to inhabit a human body, and also as one of the best artists and best poets. That notwithstanding, he has managed to remain relatively obscure in the history of Western thought.

He was against most everything: Christianity, the Church ("remove away that black'ning church"), education that taught only conformity, sin when used as an impediment to human freedom, politics, and the established order. He is often called a mystic, but he was far too active, far too hostile, and too interested in the affairs of the world to be a traditional mystic—if there is such a thing. He loved the idea of the American Revolution which he portrayed with flames cleansing the soul of mankind so people could find their own inherent humanity.

Not surprisingly, his critics described him as an "unfortunate lunatic," a "charming crank" and as one whose egregious vanity allowed him elaborate visions of how humanity should make its way in the world. Those whose stock and trade was the excoriation of sin could hardly abide one such as Blake, and they shivered when he wrote "the road of excess leads to the palace of wisdom."

Blake was essentially self-educated except in the trade of engraving to which he was apprenticed at age 14. He sought to free thought from "mind-forg'd manacles" because by shedding all of the hurdles and impediments society puts in our path, the mind could deduce our true nature, our pure self, our beauty, and our spirit.

While there is no evidence Blake ever came near a boat, he gives rowers the inspiration always to reach beyond our self-limitations. Human will is what drove him intellectually just as human will is what divides the champion from the mere competitor. He loved the human body: "And all must love the human form / In heathen, Turk or Jew /Where Mercy, Love & Pity dwell / There God is dwelling, too."

We see Blake the libertine, Blake the lover, Blake the champion of all races, and Blake the seeker after a god in human form, not some otherworldly, mean spirited landlord. We find the world through art and love and compassion for others and there are no limits on the imagination of man.

Blake's own art, for example, the engraving for the cover of his book *Songs of Innocence and of Experience*, demonstrates what was going on in his head. He preceded van Gogh by one hundred years, but the artistic debt of the latter is clear.

Unlike Augustine who argued that man needs the church for guidance, Blake sought to show that man is an independent moral and spiritual being. He looked inward to find and understand himself, and while much of what he created is obscure, much is also beautiful and sublime: "He who binds himself to a joy / Does the winged life destroy; / But he who kisses the joy as it flies / lives in eternity's sunrise."

Blake is also known for his aphorisms such as "prudence is a rich, ugly old maid, courted by incapacity." My favorite is: "Improvement makes strait roads, but the crooked roads without improvement are the roads of genius." Why do I like it? First he used the spelling for a water passage to describe a road, and second, he acknowledges that some extraordinary events and thoughts come from untraditional places. No matter how sophisticated we are, we must retain our sense of surprise and wonder.

CHAPTER 19

Drowning, Hypothermia, and Other Unpleasantries

> "The enemy is anyone who is going to get you killed, no matter which side he is on." Joseph Heller, *Catch-22*

The value of having a boat is so you don't have to swim. I *can* swim, but I'd rather not. Sometimes it just happens. I was in my single on the Willamette early morning, early spring just cruising along when I looked at my starboard keeper (the metal piece that keeps your oar in the lock) and it was open. Over I go. I swam the boat to shore and heard a car honk: a driver on the road next to the river had seen me and stopped. I waved, crawled back in and rowed back to the dock where a sheriff's car was waiting. I was very grateful to the good Samaritan who stopped and called it in. Now really, you thought-nazis, that last sentence doesn't offend the don't-end-a-sentence-in-a-preposition-at-any-cost rule, no matter what you spinach-eaters say. But it does remind me of a...

PREPOSITION JOKE

Texan is wandering around Harvard Yard and asks a student: "Can you tell me where the library is at?" Student replies: "Obviously you don't go to Harvard or you would know where the library is and you would not end a sentence in a preposition." Texan: "Well butter my butt and call me a biscuit, let me rephrase: Can you tell me where the library's at, Dickweed?"

Drowning is a deceptively quiet killer—usually no splashing, waving of arms, or shouting because our respiratory system is designed primarily for breathing and only secondarily for speech, so if there is no air in the lungs, there is no ability to call out. When in distress, the victim doesn't usually break the surface long enough to exhale, inhale, and call out. Drowning people don't wave their arms because the reflex is to spread the arms and press down on the water, and in a panic state the victim cannot move volitionally to wave or even grab a flotation device. Drowning bodies remain vertical in the water so the struggle before submersion can be as short as twenty seconds.

PHILOSOPHY TIME

Much of philosophical thought is centered on the meaning of life, and death is the big void at the end that no philosopher or theologian can describe. What is the meaning of life? That it ends. Does that take care of the problem for you? Even though no mortal can describe what it is like to be dead (kind of like the ephemeral *ding an sich*), many such as Socrates, Augustine and Kierkegaard, saw philosophy as a way of preparing for death. Kierkegaard wrote: "The highest wisdom is to live each day as if it were our last and also as the first day of a very long life." Most philosophers acknowledge the shortness of life and the juxtaposition between man as the inheritor of the earth on the one hand, and an insignificant grain of sand on the other.

Picture this: an eight full of novice rowers with a novice cox and a tug pushing a barge full of wood chips bearing down on them. This is the panic a class on the Willamette River in Portland experienced and they did not even know how to get out of the way. The tug backed down, sounding its emergency whistle about twenty times and a few rowers got in random strokes enough to avoid being run down.

In another accident caused by consummate stupidity, a couple of guys were out in a pair (one oar each) before dawn with no lights when they were overtaken by a tug pushing a barge. They felt its presence more than saw it and bailed out just before impact. They were lucky because there was no crash. The barge's bow wake rolled both the guys and the boat out of the way with no damage to person or thing. Do not try this at home.

Corvallis Rowing Club rules require a launch with a bag full of life jackets for every on-water practice. You might wonder why rowers don't routinely wear flotation devices. The answer is that they are too bulky and too hot, but that sounds kind of flimsy when drowning is the alternative. The rule is, however, that your oar is a flotation device and if the boat goes over, you stay with the boat.

A couple of high school crew boats got into trouble on the Potomac recently around Hains Point where the river is very wide and can be choppy. Unlike most venues, there were rescue and fire boats from Reagan Airport across the river to respond. Years ago, Dave Gantz and I were rowing a double just up river from where the high school crews swamped. It was one of those grey, heavy summer mornings in Washington, where the atmosphere is so laden with moisture that it is as oppressive as a congressional debate. We were under the 14th Street bridge and KABOOM, lightening hit the bridge. About the last place you want to be in an electrical storm is on the water in a boat with metal fittings. We made it back to the boathouse in record time. The prospect of death is a great motivator.

Sick Lawyer Joke

Lawyer comes in from the golf course looking wasted. His wife asks "what's the matter?" "My partner Henry dropped dead on the fifth green." "Oh, that's terrible. I am so sorry for you." "Yeah. All the rest of the way around it was hit the ball, drag Henry, hit the ball, drag Henry."

At the 2010 Worlds regatta a fierce wind kicked up on the third morning and at least one four went over. (Using all of my philosophical skills, I deduced that from the fact that the rescue boat brought in four sweep oars.) Of course, they could have saved the oars and left the people—who knows.

A single sculler told me that the woman in the lane next to hers flipped on the second stroke and she herself was so terrified that when she finally made it back to the dock she trembled for the next half hour. After multiple delays, the head official announced that racing for the rest of the day was "abandoned."

Rowing in cold weather presents its own set of dangers. If the combined temperature of the water and air is under 80 degrees, hypothermia can set in within two minutes if your boat goes over and you are in the water. Most clubs have specific rules such as the four oar rule: no launching in air temperatures under 40 degrees Fahrenheit unless there are four oars in play—either a double or a four. All rowers must wear fabrics that insulate when wet (i.e., not cotton).

Hypothermia happens when the body cannot keep up with heat loss so that the metabolism slows and the person does not have enough heat energy to function. Thinking becomes muddled, speech confused, muscles clumsy. Body temperature of 95 degrees, less than four degrees below normal, is a medical emergency and can lead to death if not promptly treated. Getting the rowers out of the water quickly is paramount. The coach should always carry a cell phone and if, for some reason they cannot be quickly extracted, they should get as much of their bodies up on the hull as possible because the heat loss of the submerged body is twenty-five times greater.

Summer is the prime drowning time. When the weather gets hot, out come the rafters and the tube drifters and the canoe paddlers, many lubricated with alcohol and their life jackets, if they have them, are in the bottom of the boat. A canoe, in particular, is very tricky to maneuver on a fast moving river, particularly if there are log snags. So the boat hits a snag, or the snag pops the tube and the person is swept under the log and caught by the river teeth (those sharp, broken off branches next to the trunk), and the rescue folks pull another body out of the river.

Accidents on the water are just that: accidents and by definition they can happen any time. Preparation and planning can reduce accidents—like maybe get out of your boat or tube and scout the rapids before you try to go through them. At the San Diego Crew Classic one year I saw the Navy coxswain steer into a UCLA boat. It was an accident, I guess.

NAVY JOKE

On night maneuvers running without lights, a destroyer received an urgent message from the Admiral. A seaman brought it to the bridge and the Captain said: "Read it out loud." The seaman hesitated, swallowed, and read: "You brainless imbecile, you nearly rammed my flagship." The Captain replied: "Very well; take it below and have it decoded."

CHAPTER 20

Friedrich Nietzsche (1844–1900)

"We have art so we do not die of the truth." Nietzsche

Friedrich Nietzsche is THE philosopher for rowers. He is the champion of the superman and of the will to power. He sees strength as the ultimate virtue and weakness as the greatest fault. For him the formula for greatness is not just to bear up under every necessity, but to love doing it. If ever there were an argument for forty-five more minutes on the erg, that is it.

Unfortunately, Nietzsche, like Thomas Jefferson, engaged in wild ideological walk-abouts. You need a quote to support your position—any position? Nietzsche will serve one up. He might even serve one up that will support both your proposition and the opposite all in one delicious and unintelligible portion.

Just to show that philosophy and life can tolerate inconsistency, look at the way I am randomly shifting tenses in these paragraphs. It seems to work better that way because philosophy, and particularly that of Nietzsche, is both historical and alive. It exists in the past and the present at the same time.

ROWTON

He is just too lazy to go back and correct it. But he does make a point: humans are really good at justifying almost anything.

His is not a systematic philosophy flowing logically from one proposition to the next. He is a poet philosopher writing in aphorisms—short pithy statements leaving one to ponder whether this is profound or stupid. He managed to be a genius and a madman at the same time. He served as an inspiration for such wildly diverse persons as Sigmund Freud and Adolf Hitler.

In his early years Nietzsche was an aspiring musician, enthralled with the genius of Richard Wagner. Wagner's operas, and particularly the four that comprise *The Ring of the Nieblungen*, have been as seminal to modern opera as Nietzsche's writings have been to modern philosophy. (By the way, it is Wagner's ring cycle, not as I have heard it referred to by the uninitiated,

Wagner's rinse cycle.) What resonated so profoundly with Nietzsche in Wagner's music was its neo-pagan setting that, by the intoxication of myth, set Germany free from what he saw as the sniffling pall of Christianity. He embraced the themes of fate, loyalty, violent emotion, and blood lust.

Humans, Nietzsche argues, need myths, illusions, and mystic intuition because the overarching human drive is the will to power. We cannot deny cruelty because it is present in the most benign manifestations such as the Christian Saints. He attacks and obliterates God, free will, human purpose, morality, world order and evil, wiping the slate clean for the arrival of his cosmic guide, Zarathustra. Modeled after Zoraster, the Persian poet and prophet 1,000 years dead, Zarathustra is Nietzsche's mouthpiece, alter ego, avatar, and press secretary.

In ten day frenzies of inspiration, Nietzsche whipped out each of the first three sections of *Thus Spoke Zarathustra*. A fourth section is in prose, not aphorisms. Nietzsche found the public little interested in the completed product, finally self-publishing it, giving away seven copies and selling forty. (It is said, without attribution, that three went to folks in Texas.) No one took much notice except to ridicule the ravings of a lunatic.

Undaunted, Nietzsche proclaimed that there are two kinds of philosophers: those like Kant who analyze the world as it is and try to make sense of it; and Nietzsche himself who legislates and brings the world into being by his own command. Adding megalomania to his list of personality disorders, he declared: "I am strong enough to break the history of mankind in two. Henceforth all philosophy will be categorized as before Nietzsche and after Nietzsche."

So Zarathustra comes down from the meditative mountain and obliterates God. Actually, God laughs himself to death. Since the people have no more need for God, they need an Ubermensch—a superman. So Nietzsche has created a new god in his own image and, with his theory of "eternal recurrence," all things return and presto, he is immortal.

To show that all thought is cyclical, or that Nietzsche was cribbing from Plato, or that Nietzsche took seriously what Plato was just chucking out there for discussion, look at Plato's dialogue *Gorgias* (and this is not a footnote) where Callicles says that morality is a farce to protect the weak. He who would truly live ought to allow his desires to wax to the uttermost. The many cannot do this. The ruler is a superman. The strong do what they can and the weak suffer what they must. Plato may have been channeling Socrates, but Nietzsche was definitely reprising Plato. Add shameless borrowing to Nietzsche's sack full of personality defects.

Rowton

Amateurs borrow; professionals steal; scholars interpret; students fantasize.

Actually Nietzsche was also attracted to the pre-Socratic Greek philosophers, against whom Plato railed. Nietzsche locked on to the concept of Agonis—that one develops his natural abilities by contests and altruism is just an excuse for not proving oneself in the game. You rowers out there in the sideways rain rowing 'til dark can know for sure that Nietzsche loves you.

The goal of human endeavor then is not the namby pamby greatest good for the masses. It is the elevation and development of superior individuals. Not unlike Plato, Nietzsche sees this happening through education and selective breeding—eugenics. Man should not be allowed to marry for love. He doesn't want the superman to be marrying the dull normal ragpicker. In fact, Nietzsche has nary a good word to say about females anywhere. One more personality zit.

It makes one shudder, but here is what Nietzsche is aiming for: "A herd of blond beasts of prey, a race of conquerors and masters, with military organization...unscrupulously placing their fearful paws upon a population perhaps vastly superior in numbers..."

He had no use for democracy and its reliance on the masses. He said, "he who cannot lie does not know what the truth is." Likewise, feminism, socialism, and anarchy are all social fungi. The ideal society is divided into three classes: producers such as farmers and merchants; officials including soldiers and functionaries; and rulers. This is, by the way, roughly the same class structure that existed during the High Middle Ages. Order is kept by the will to power which is ruthless and constant.

It is tempting to write the guy off as a vicious nut case, and his thinking, or in some cases ranting, is subject to many criticisms which I will address in a minute. But he does what a philosopher should do: he makes us think. He knocks out all the props from what we believe and dares us to reassemble the pieces.

So for rowers in particular, listen to what Zarathustra is saying about war and warriors and then think of what your coach is telling you. I have sometimes substituted the word race or racing for war or battle.

> My brothers in racing! I love you from the very heart. I am, and have always been your kind. And I am also your best enemy. So let me tell you the truth.

I see many soldiers (rowers): if only I could see many warriors; what they wear is called a uniform: may what they conceal with it not be uniform, too!

I do not exhort you to work, but to battle…. May your work be a battle, may your peace be a victory.

They call you heartless: but your heart is true, and I love the modesty of your kind-heartedness. You feel ashamed of your flow, while others feel ashamed of their ebb.

Let your nobility show itself in obeying.

Thus spoke Zarathustra.

The human will is the will to power. But only for the superman.

The ignorant, to be sure, the people—they are like a river down which a boat swims; and in the boat, solemn and disguised, sit the assessments of value.

You put your will and your values upon the river of becoming; what the people believe to be good and evil betrays to me an ancient will to power.

But wherever I found living creatures, there too I heard the language of obedience. All living creatures are obeying creatures.

He who cannot obey himself will be commanded. That is the nature of living creatures.

And life itself told me this secret; 'Behold' it said, 'I am that *which must overcome itself again and again*.'

God has died and now we desire that the superman shall live.

Thus spoke Zarathustra.

The criticisms of Nietzsche's work roll down like thunder, not the least of which is that it inspired the scourge of Nazism, genocide, and sanctified cruelty. His methods of the study of words and genetics are laughably without historical perspective or accuracy. Lack of evidence never stopped him from bold assertions, and indeed, evidence itself was completely irrelevant when he was looking to myth and intuition.

Nietzsche's one dimensional human leaves out, or at least minimizes, human emotion, human desires, and social instincts. What he postulates as the superman is imaginary and the society that that figure commands is unlivable. But here is the great big BUT when it comes to Nietzsche. He really did shake up Western philosophy and he was right in at least one particular: there is a before and after Nietzsche, and every philosopher since has had to deal with him. Reading his work makes us struggle with the very questions of what our lives are about. That is his genius even if he was an antisocial nut.

One more aphorism before we leave Nietzsche: "Insanity is the exception in individuals. In groups, parties, peoples and times, it is the rule." And finally, just to show that self-knowledge, while the goal, is an effervescent finish line, he said: "How can man know himself? He is a dark and hidden thing.

CHAPTER 21

Coaches and Coxswains

> "Rowing is the only sport that originated as a form of capital punishment." Anon.

Coaches think they own you. Is it dark? Is it windy, and cold and raining? Have you already burned enough calories to heat Philadelphia? No matter. Another piece is good and at the end of that piece another couple of minutes and at the end of those minutes another hard twenty and at the end of that, there might just be enough time for another piece. And then you get to carry a 300-pound eight to the boat house and do five sets of jumpies.

Coaches call this "finding the edge of your potential," and the sport really demands it because racing requires that you reach your anaerobic threshold in the first few strokes of a race and anaerobic work is nineteen times harder than aerobic, which means for the next 225 strokes of a college race you are operating on nothing but guts.

Coach Philosophy

Successful coaches, not just in rowing but in all sports, are teachers, and one of the all-time greats was John Wooden. His UCLA basketball teams won eighty-eight straight games and ten national titles. Duke's coach Mike Krzyzewski said of Wooden: "You can have a pretty good argument about who is the second greatest college coach of all time. There is absolutely no argument about who is the greatest."

What made Wooden such a great coach is that he taught the fundamentals for life and basketball. Here is some of his wisdom, compiled over his ninety-nine years of life:

> Ability is a poor man's wealth.

> Don't let what you cannot do interfere with what you can.

If you don't have time to do it right, when will you have time to do it over?

Never mistake activity for achievement.

Talent is God-given. Be humble. Fame is man-given. Be grateful. Conceit is self-given. Be careful.

Be far more concerned with your character than your reputation, he said, and remember that it is what you learn after you know it all that counts.

OCCAM'S RAZOR

We're not talking about a three headed Norelco electric here. William of Ockham (spelling was a lot more fluid in the fourteenth century) was a Franciscan monk who got himself ex-communicated by Pope John XXII for impure thoughts. Occam in turn declared the pope a heretic, which usually was a head-removing mistake. Occam's philosophical principle, like that of many great coaches today, was to cut out all unnecessary baggage: "The more perfect a nature, the fewer means it requires for its operation." This "principle of parsimony" means cut out the superfluous, the distractions, the BS, and the razmataz. Occam's razor translates into "keep it simple, stupid" but is a lot classier.

PAIN

Aeschylus, fittingly the father of Greek tragedy wrote: "There is advantage in the wisdom won from pain." In some sports, like football, you may suffer pain from a particularly hard hit. In rowing, you know, with an assurance that surpasses all understanding, that you WILL suffer pain. In doing so, you will learn about many things, not the least of which is yourself. If there is one goal above all others in life-long education, it is self-knowledge. Here the roles of philosophy and rowing exactly coincide.

What makes rowing pain fun pain, to coin an oxymoron to go with the likes of deliberate speed, jumbo shrimp, proud humility and military justice, is its mystical cloak where the true nature of the beast is more felt than seen, intuited than known. You can't know rowing unless you have met, confronted and conquered the pain.

Coach Robert Valerian said: "I can teach 90% of the rowing stroke in ten minutes. The other 10% will require you a lifetime of effort to learn." He probably means that ever elusive *ding an sich*. What are the imponderables that make one boat surge and glide while another is hammering the water with its oars and killing the fish? Why do otherwise normal people get up at 5 a.m. and row to exhaustion, facing backwards while ripping the skin off their hands? It is a mystery.

Philosophical Moment

Epistemology is the theory of knowledge—how we know what we know. I can tell you that the older I get, the less I think I know. Some call it senility; I prefer to think of it as a form of wisdom. Philosopher David Hume thought we could know by observing and most modern scientists would certainly concur. (There is, however, an increasingly popular strain of factless science that holds that the world shall be as we want it to be, the evidence be damned. My mother often subscribed to this theory.)

The enlightenment, that spawned our nation's founding ideology, relied on reason and up to the carnage of the First World War, many thought reason and science could eradicate the scruffier human traits that had retarded progress. Now, it takes a particularly robust form of myopia to overlook genocide, hunger, environmental degradation, poverty, and ignorance to conclude that Camelot is just around the corner.

A rower's epistemology is a combination of science and mysticism. We know our bodies because we spend so much time training muscle memory, expanding our endurance and building strength. We learn to listen to what our bodies tell us, particularly when we are hurt or are harming ourselves. But we also learn to drown out, ignore or override our body's shrieking complaints and to muscle through to the finish.

How do we do this? How do we know we won't die? From where comes the inner resolve of the champion? No theory of knowledge can tell us, nor for that matter, can any religion. On the water salvation is by works, not faith. Epistemology has yet to crack the mysterious nut called the mind of a winner.

Coxswains

A swain is a servant, and that may be the origin of the name coxswain—a person whose job it was to steer the boat. Or it may come from the cock who is crowing out the commands, for all I know. Whatever the origin, the cox is the coach in the boat, and a good cox can make a huge difference. A former Olympic cox figured out the set problem in a four I was in (not at the Olympics, of course) in about three strokes. Craig Tokuda, our cox the first year we won at the Head of the Charles, walked the entire course figuring his angles for every turn. His perfect course is even more remarkable when you consider that the previous two nights he had slept on a chair and ottoman in "boys town," the hotel room into which four of us were crammed. Besides two beds, the room had a roll away in the short entry hall in front of the bathroom. Its unfortunate occupant got his head stepped on each time one of our aged bladders required a visit to the john.

When to sprint, how to motivate, and indeed, what can be said to either inspire or to calm a rower—that is the challenge and the genius of a good coxswain. The coxswain, more than anyone else, is in charge of making the boat perform as a team. It is, in short, a hell of a lot more than steering the boat. The nasty and pretty much discredited practice of throwing the cox in the water after the race has diminished, primarily because much of the water on which rowing is done is toxic. The garbage and chemicals and twinky wrappers are just what you can see, but lurking therein are all sorts of noxious skin diseases: a veritable dermatologist's smorgasbord. The best that can be said for dunking the cox is that if you are inclined to do it, you probably won.

THE SETTLE

Paradoxically, sometimes in rowing you go faster by going slower. "Settle" is a command to lengthen the stroke and sometimes reduce the rate to increase the run of the boat (the distance it goes with each stroke). In a race, with the adrenaline rush, sometimes it takes two or three settles to get the boat swinging. Sometimes it doesn't happen at all and the fish are abraded and annoyed. Rowing is a rhythm sport, and the speed achieved depends on the synchronization of all that power. If it looks and feels like a samba, you lose; if it feels like a waltz you get the laurel wreath.

One piece of coaching advice is eternal: the boat is not made up of individuals. It is a unit and it will not succeed unless it functions as one. Here Nietzsche's superman is not much help. One person cannot row the boat by himself. It is like an orchestra where each player must do her part, play in tune, follow the conductor. This requires trust, and support for each other. The best thing that can be said for a rower is that she makes everyone in the boat row better. No matter what the individual abilities in a boat, at the end of a race either everyone or no one gets a medal.

The eleventh-century French epic, *Song of Roland* is instructive here. Roland is charged with guarding the rear of Charlemagne's troops as they head out of what is now Spain. He is given an oliphant (horn) to blow if he needs help, but when he is ambushed by the Saracens (Muslims), he thinks he can handle it all by himself and refuses to blow until all is lost. He then blows so hard that his temples burst and he dies, along with his troops. Charlemagne returns and drives the invaders into the river where they drown. It is a cautionary tale about trying to do it all yourself (as if you hadn't figured that out).

CHAPTER 22

Kierkegaard (1813–1855)

"The heart has reasons which the reason knows not of." Pascal

While Kierkegaard and Nietzsche are both loosely categorized as existentialists, they couldn't be more different in what they construct as the ideal human. For Nietzsche, it is the superman; for Kierkegaard, the individual who is right with God. Both distrust the masses. They are cannon fodder for Nietzsche's superman, and the source of untruth for Kierkegaard's God focused individual.

When Kierkegaard died at age forty-two, Nietzsche was eleven years old. Their philosophies did not compete because Kierkegaard's homilies and self-critical musings received scant attention until the twentieth century.

Kierkegaard's writings seek to unsettle the individual by looking inward and stripping away all of the detritus that society puts upon us. He recognized how difficult that is, particularly when the exercise demands costly action from the individual. But that is what individual responsibility is about. The individual must be separated from the crowd and come face to face with God. Only when standing naked before God, with all of the pretense and societal veneer stripped away, can remorse and repentance happen. Thus ethics and morality are not creations of society, but creations of God as perceived by the enlightened individual. A personality is ripe only when man has made the truth his own and that truth is God's truth.

Kierkegaard's purpose in writing is to label the blind alleys, unmask the deception, and call out the hypocrisy that the crowd (society) uses to separate the individual from God. A crowd is untruth, he says, because it renders the individual impenitent and irresponsible. Thus loving one's neighbor is self-denial and while traditionally that was thought to be morally right, it displaces the focus from God to man. Making the crowd the authority in matters of truth may lead to material success and other earthly advantages, but it is an abdication of individual responsibility, a fountain of untruth, and a sink of cowardice.

All of this seems, to our eyes, to be thin gruel for nourishing the love of philosophy, but keep in mind that the resurgence in interest in Kierkegaard came after World Wars where the superman, the crowd and the advance of human civilization all appeared to be bankrupt. The lesson, or at least a lesson, is that the appeal of a particular thinker may depend on what else is happening in the world, and a philosophy that sustains one generation may not resonate with another. Clearly, Nietzsche's exuberant declaration that God was dead was wrong, God demonstrating remarkable regenerative powers.

I came across a short novel of Kierkegaard's entitled *Repetition* and thought he might be speaking directly to rowers. Alas, it is about unrequited love, and not the kind of training necessary to win races. Ah, but there is another Kierkegaard quote written especially for rowers: "health and salvation can only be found in motion."

CHAPTER 23

Famous Crabs

"All we keep of the truth is what we give away." Sam Hazo, poet

Catching a crab is like dropping the baton in a relay race, fumbling the football, dribbling the basketball off your foot. It stops the run in the boat as if someone had thrown out an anchor, and in a lot of ways, that is exactly right.

Here is what happens: the oar is not completely squared up as it enters the water, so it tends to dive, and because the oar is so deep, the rower cannot get it out of the water at the release, but the boat keeps moving so the oar handle hits the rower in the chest and unceremoniously lifts him off his seat and out of the boat.

The alternative, if the rower is quick enough, is that he lays all the way back and the oar handle passes over, hopefully not hitting him in the chin, and ends up behind him. Tough to row that way. The boat is now in disarray, both because of the sudden stop and because the offending oar is alongside the boat and the rower behind cannot row with it there, so the oar has to be retrieved, the swimmer rescued, and as far as the race goes, you are yesterday's lunch.

CRABBING AND PHILOSOPHY

There is crabbing and then there is crabbing—where you try to catch those tasty crustaceans on purpose. Crabbing on the Oregon coast is wonderful and my crabbing companions on Yaquina Bay were Tom, in his early 80s and Robert, in his early 90s. Both were schooled in philosophy, music, religion, law, politics, women and just about everything else worth talking about. So a day of crabbing consisted of hooking up Robert's boat, launching it at Sawyers Landing, motoring up to a likely looking spot, like buoy 14, dropping in the crab pots, pouring a cup of coffee, and discussing Hegel and Kant for twenty minutes. We then would pull up the pots to see if we had scored. Now that is sport for you.

On a good day (and the best crabbing months are those late in the year that end in the letter r) we each limit out with a dozen, Sawyers cooked them (at a hard boil for 17 minutes), we cleaned them much to the delight of the ever-present seagulls, and we had a feast with our wives, lots of salad, melted butter, and wine. Life is good. And, the philosophical problems we solved on the water were fresh and demanding of our attention the next time we went out. It is like only needing one book.

Rowton

Cook the crab inside your own house, and you'll have to tear it down. El stinko. Cook it outside and your neighbors will tear down your house for you.

Back to the Ugly Kind of Crab

In a single, a crab will flip you unless you lean hard away from it as soon as you feel your oar start to grab. The hardest part of learning in a single is having the confidence to really drive hard with your legs when your balance is iffy, and I don't know any pre-packaged way to gain confidence other than by doing it, and having a good and patient coach to improve your technique. You will get wet. I guarantee it.

A partial crab or crabette is when your oar catches as it comes out of the water, but not enough to dive and stop the boat. It just ruins the run, makes the recovery jerky, and generally mucks things up. In really rough water when you are smacking into waves with your oar blade on the recovery, it is like having a crabette on every stroke. That kind of race never seems to end. But if you feel your oar start to grab, you have to loosen your grip and the water will usually pop the oar out.

Paraphilosophy

Like the crabette, paraphilosophy is the art of half-assed mental work we so commonly encounter in most everything. That is why I like rowing. There are no short cuts. If your strength, stamina, and technique are inadequate, you will lose. Simple.

But in mental work, we are often unprepared in strength, stamina and technique. Here is an example: the best speakers I know practice, prepare meticulously, keep their presentations short and know precisely what they are going to say. When did you last hear such a speaker? Ever? Most speakers, and unfortunately some who speak all the time, don't rehearse, don't know what they are going to say, don't say it well, and bore us out of our socks.

Since when was winging it in the world of the mind acceptable when winging it in the world of rowing won't fly? If there is one clear outcome desired from all education it is that of mental discipline. Mental discipline does not wing it.

The Danger of Billed Caps

As long as we are talking about disasters large and small, let me warn of loading boats on a trailer while wearing a billed cap. Transporting racing shells is an ordeal since the eights are sixty feet long. The trailers that hold these puppies have metal arms that stick out at levels of about four feet, seven feet, and ten feet so the boats can be transported in three or more tiers. Getting the boats on the top level requires that several rowers stand up on the trailer to help guide the boat to the top while a bunch of others heft it up from below. One of our rowers saw that more people were needed above and jumped up on the trailer, but because of his billed cap did not see that he was jumping into an arm of the trailer with his head. Forty-two stitches later, he returned from the emergency room, and he raced the next day with blood still in his hair. The philosophical point here is...well, there isn't one. Yes, there is. The existentialists tell us we learn from our own experience and he was wearing his hat backwards last time we loaded.

The San Diego Crew Classic is a college and masters race that is a pleasure for northern crews who have been rowing with ice all around. Corvallis Rowing Club sent a women's masters crew a few years ago made up of our best rowers. For masters, a 2,000-meter race, particularly early in the year, is a real challenge. Our women were doing fine until an oar popped out of the lock. Killer. They got it back in and soldiered on, but the race was lost. So at the beginning of every race we compulsively check the wing nuts on our foot stretchers, the locks on our keepers to make sure the oar stays in, and some even empty out their water bottles to lighten the load.

A lot of crabs happen because the rower has a death grip on the oar handle. Not only will this cause big blisters, tired forearms, and bad technique, but it prevents the oar from finding the right depth in the water and pulling through smoothly. In golf it was said that Walter Hagen had the perfect grip and never got a blister. I have heard of no such thing in rowing. But legendary golfer Sam Snead had it right when he said: "If a lot of people gripped a knife and fork the way they grip a golf club, they would starve to death."

So the philosophical question is: to tape or not to tape? My approach is to let my hands get hamburgered up at the start of the on-water season so the calluses will form and be done with it. This isn't a mantra, though, like vegetarianism or rooting for the Cubs. I will tape a particularly offensive blister, but I think routine taping just means you will have to keep taping—like wearing one of those soft cervical collars that keeps your neck from healing. Rowing in the rain will rip the skin off your hands, no matter how many calluses. I could make some philosophical comment about rain and renewal and blisters. But I won't.

CHAPTER 24

Sartre (1905–1980)

> "Thinking instead of acting is the number one golf disease." Sam Snead, an existentialist without knowing it

Jean-Paul Sartre's Communist-based existentialism cost him his friendship with Camus, but gave him a platform from which to cast spitballs at religion, other forms of existentialism, and most other philosophical thinkers. He is a systematic in the sense that he explains his form of existentialism—how the parts fit together—and defends it against its multiple critics.

Against the charge that existentialism dwells in despair, self-deception, and all that is ignoble in humans, Sartre doesn't flinch. Yes, he says, we are hypocrites and we lie to ourselves because we realize, although we won't admit, that we fall short of being sincere. But existentialism is a doctrine that renders human life possible, affirms truth and action, jettisons any *a priori* or revealed knowledge, banishes God, and makes humans responsible for their actions. Thus, he argues, it is the ultimate ethical system.

Sartre the man, as opposed to Sartre the philosopher, loved the United States, particularly its jazz, cinema, and literature. I can imagine Hemmingway and Sartre quaffing a few martinis together, although I read recently that a Hemmingway martini was 2 oz. whereas one you get today is more likely to be 6 oz. Inflation, I guess. Sartre and Hemmingway actually did meet once, in Cuba. Apparently the conversation was not an intellectual blockbuster.

The starting point for existentialism is that existence comes before essence. Forget about God or any creation myths, man is, in the Cartesian sense that he thinks, and it is from man's actions that his essence is known. Man is alone in having his existence before his essence. An artisan thinks of the shape and function of a knife before he creates it, but with man, we know him (his essence) only through his actions. Thus each individual defines himself, is responsible for himself, and is without excuse (such as blaming bad actions on some preordained force like original sin).

Sartre doesn't spend much energy on where man came from—he simply is. But because each man is responsible for his own actions, he is also responsible

92

for all of humankind. He chooses for himself, and in so doing, chooses for all men. "Nothing can be better for us unless it is better for all." This, again, is pretty close to the golden rule, present in virtually all moral systems, although the committed existentialist would shiver at the thought.

Anguish comes from this realization that in choosing for himself, he is choosing for all of his fellow humans. It is unsettling and difficult because man must act but the options are never clear and the negative consequences are present no matter what course he chooses (and choosing not to choose is a choice anyway).

Man is abandoned because God does not exist and thus cannot toss out a life ring in the form of moral orders. Man is "condemned to be free" and without excuse. And man lives with despair because he must rely on his own resources and there is no hope for a reliable or pain free outcome. While others criticize this as pessimistic, dour, and depressing, Sartre says what they really are criticizing is the vigor of his optimism because both the hero and the coward are defined only by the sum total of their deeds, not by their aspirations, their rhetoric, or their intentions.

As to the non-existence of God, the existentialist does not exhaust himself in proving that God does not exist because it doesn't matter. All that matters is that only man can save himself and this, says Sartre, is totally optimistic.

Philosophy can be done through stories, and Sartre is a master storyteller. In *The Wall* a rebel in the Spanish Civil War is captured. He is told that he will be put up against the wall and shot in the morning, and in contemplating his imminent death, he loses all sense of his humanity. His comrades are taken out and shot, but he is interrogated further and told if he gives up his leader, he will be spared. He knows where the man is but gives a false location (a cemetery keeper's shack). They come back and he is removed from the ranks of the condemned. He learns that his leader felt unsafe where he was hiding and went to the cemetery keeper's shack. What does it mean? Life is absurd—that is a start. We all can ponder the rest of it.

The existentialist nonsermon for the rower is that you are judged not by your aspirations, or your big talk, or even your coach's high praise, but by what you do on the water. Since what you choose for yourself you choose for all men, if you are dogging it in practice, that is what you are inflicting on your whole team. So buckle down, sucka.

CHAPTER 25

Stamina and the Stoics

> "Evils are not punishment but are paternal corrections like exercise is to the athlete." Seneca the Stoic

Rob Hannah, then a junior at Oregon State and one of their strongest rowers, was having kind of a slow summer around the boat house. The year before he had discovered a mysterious twenty-eight-inch iron bell under the dock that, with substantial engineering aplomb, he and some friends floated up (using those big commercial water dispenser bottles). How did a half-ton bell get under the dock? A newspaper story produced no clues, but Rob did manage also to scavenge up pieces of railroad rails, bike frames, a moped.... No such excitement in the summer of '09.

So he decided to row 100,000 meters on the ergometer. All at once. To break the world record. Crazy.

Let's review before tackling this exhausting event. Masters row 1,000 meter pieces because they approximate a race. You row as hard as you can for as long as it takes (between three and four minutes probably). Two thousand-meter pieces are the stock and trade of college rowers, and both masters and college do 5,000-meter pieces because those approximate a head race. But 100,000 meters? That's almost sixty miles—two and one half times a marathon. Nuts.

How did he prepare? The night before he "ate a big dinner and went to bed early." Well, he did a bit more than that. About a month before the big day he started doing between 100,000 and 150,000 meters a week, and a week before he did a 50,000-meter test run. The butt turned out to be the Achilles heel, to mix both a metaphor and body parts. That meant a good butt pad taped on to the erg seat was a must. The butt, Rob reported, starts to really feel it at about 30,000 meters—like sitting on sharp rocks.

Rob's coxswain, Stefan, was with him through the whole six and one half grueling hours and six other rowers paced him on adjoining ergs for most of the way. Stefan fed him water, Gatorade, power bars, and half a banana as he was rowing, hitting his mouth some of the time.

Philosophical Update

When we think enduring pain and liking it we think of the stoics of whom Seneca, a first-century Spaniard transplanted to Rome, is foremost. Stoic philosophy held that man must be indifferent to "externals" so that he can be happy under any circumstances and endure any of life's disruptions. Seneca said that no one is more unhappy than one who has never met adversity and thus has not tested himself.

Rowton

Seneca was all for jollying it up with a glass of wine or two, but apparently not to the point of feeling no pain, since pain is good. I think Seneca is like Sartre because, no matter what they say about themselves and their beliefs, they depress the hell out of me.

Just to show that hypocrisy is not a new invention, Seneca, in his own life, was pretty much the opposite of what he preached in his philosophy. As a lawyer, he amassed a substantial fortune, reportedly by lending money at usurious rates. While he argued that we must avoid being influenced by material things, he owned 500 tables with fruitwood tops and ivory legs upon which he served feasts and banquets.

His reputation as an orator and writer was such that Emperor Caligula in about 37 CE thought he should be killed. Caligula was as bloodthirsty as they come, but he refrained from doing so only because Seneca's poor health suggested he would soon die naturally. Then he was banished to Corsica by Claudius in 41 CE, was restored by Agrippina in 49 CE and became a tutor to Nero, who became Emperor in 54 CE. After about five years Nero slouched into tyranny and some pretty dysfunctional bursts of homicide. Seneca was invited to take his own life which he did most theatrically in 65 CE. Writers of Elizabethan tragedy (Shakespeare and Ben Johnson, for example) were influenced by the flamboyant way in which Seneca departed this pale.

So while Rob was toiling away on his erg, thinking his butt was on fire, he no doubt took consolation in Seneca's advice that "no situation is so harsh that a dispassionate mind cannot find some consolation in it." Stoicism emphasized oneness with nature, the ascendancy of reason, and playing the hand that you are dealt in life. Seneca was pretty good with a turn of the phrase. Here are some of them:

> For self-knowledge, testing is necessary.

In disaster is virtue's opportunity.

By suffering misfortune the mind grows able to belittle suffering.

What can happen to somebody can happen to anybody.

It is more civilized to laugh at life than to lament over it.

So deeply rooted is the vice of depending on public opinion that so simple a thing as grief is subject to counterfeiting.

The life of many people is a fiction polished up for exhibition.

The mind must have relaxation, and will rise stronger and keener after recreation.

Back to the ordeal of Rob Hannah; at 75,000 meters his knees felt like jello, his butt was fried, and his mind was in the lost and found, but he kept on, quoting Seneca (not really) and with 1,500 meters to go he began to walk his split down (go faster) so that by the last 400 meters he was doing a 1:26 split. What that means is that every stroke he was pulling after six and one half hours is harder that any stroke I can pull ever. He beat the record by more than nine minutes. A giant among pygmies.

Just a few more comments on Seneca: he recommended that adults give up the active life in favor of philosophic contemplation. Just goes to show that not everything fits. In mockery, he said: "It used to be a Greek aberration to inquire into the number of Ulysses' rowers…"

Rowton

What is the matter with that? How many did he have?

Another Homily of Pain

After a periodic 2,000-meter test, one of our rowers wrote the twelve steps of rowing a 2K which I reproduce here without adulteration or permission:

1. I admitted my legs are powerless—I am 1,200 meters into a 2K.

2. I have come to believe only a power greater than myself can get me through this piece.

3. Made a decision to turn my breathing over to God 'cause I sure as hell can't breath on my own right now.

4. Made a searching and fearless moral inventory of my skill deficits.

5. Admitted to God, myself and another person that I was the one that crabbed in the high 15.

6. Was entirely ready to have God remove me from my seat.

7. Humbly pleaded with God to remove me from my seat.

8. Made a list of all persons I had harmed and became willing to make amends to them all.

9. Made a list of all of my possessions and decided who would get what, since I obviously am going to die.

10. Desperately begged God to remove me from my seat.

11. Sought through prayer and meditation an understanding of what heinous crime I had committed that this third 500 should be my penance.

12. Having had a spiritual awakening as a result of crossing the finish line, tried to carry this message to other rowers.

Any similarity to the twelve steps of Alcoholics Anonymous is purely coincidental.

CHECKING IN ON THE BIBLE

What we have been talking about in this chapter is, in the parlance of the Good Book, steadfastness. It was a favorite word of the almost-apostle Paul in writing to various constituencies such as the Corinthians. He meant steadfastness in the faith, but the same condition of immovability and dedication applies to rowing.

The word is also used in the book of Job and if anybody's trials exceeded those of Rob Hannah, Job would be my candidate.

Since we are totally out of chronological order here talking about the Stoics in the midst of the existentialists, I will attempt to make a connection. The first is the aphorisms—the witty or wise sayings that, hopefully, make us think. Erasmus brought these into the modern world and Nietzsche used them extensively. The second connection that we owe to the Stoics is the concept of Natural Law. The Stoics believed in a rational world order that was superior to the passions and appetites of humans.

Many of the aphorisms suggest (preach?) that man can, by reason, live in harmony with the natural world. Here are a bunch from the first-century Stoic, Epictetus:

> Wealth consists not in having great possessions, but in having few wants.
>
> We have two ears and one mouth so that we can listen twice as much as we speak. (Zeno of Citium said the same.)
>
> It is not what happens to you but how you react that matters. Eleanor Roosevelt is also credited with this quote as is Aldous Huxley. Goes to show that the recycling of ideas is good for the intellectual environment.
>
> If you want to improve, be content to be thought foolish and stupid.
>
> Only the educated are free.
>
> Make the best use of what is in your power and take the rest as it happens.
>
> Silence is safer than speech.
>
> It is impossible to begin to learn that which one thinks one already knows.
>
> It is hardship that shows what man is.

And finally, since philosophy is action based on rational thought, Epictetus' definition of philosophy: "a man should so live that his happiness shall depend as little as possible on external things."

I don't know if Rob was happy after his 100,000 meters, but I am sure he was hungry.

CHAPTER 26

Ludwig Wittgenstein (1889–1951)

> "Bad philosophers are like slumlords. It is my job to put them out of business." Wittgenstein

Rude. Rude and mouthy and arrogant. And maybe dangerous, with a fireplace poker in his hand. That is a description of the twentieth-century philosopher that, by fellow philosophers in 1999, was ranked among the five most influential in history: Plato, Aristotle, Kant, Nietzsche, and Wittgenstein. He dismissed Cambridge University's famous philosopher G. E. Moore as being an example of how far a person could get in life with absolutely no intelligence whatsoever. He thought reading the dialogues of Socrates a "frightful waste of time."

The fireplace poker incident happened at King's College, Cambridge in October, 1946 at a meeting of the Cambridge Moral Science Club where Karl Popper, another Austrian philosopher, was the invited guest speaker. Popper argued that history does not progress, but rather moves in fits and starts through trial and error, but there are discoverable moral truths, and democracy is the best form of organization in which to pursue the search. (Just to show that all who love philosophy are not in the ivory tower, one of Popper's disciples is the billionaire businessman and philanthropist, George Soros.)

Wittgenstein, on the other hand, held that philosophers make up these metaphysical constructs that have nothing to do with things as they really are—they are on "frictionless ice," cut off from their place in the real world. For Wittgenstein there are no philosophical systems or problems, only language games. A language game (which, by the way, he made up the rules for and was the consummate player) was a way of discovering what we mean when we use words in a particular context, at a particular time and with particular grammar. When we scrub up language this way, the philosophical problems and constructs go away. It is philosophy's job to free us from our self-imposed confusion over the language we use.

So Popper is addressing the Moral Science Club and Wittgenstein is standing by the fireplace heckling. The exchange about the fundamental purpose of philosophy gets heated with the two heavyweight brains slugging it out, and

100

finally Wittgenstein challenges Popper to state a valid moral principle and Popper retorts: "thou shall not threaten the guest speaker with a fireplace poker." Wittgenstein stalks out. High drama in the world of philosophy.

Wittgenstein wrote a book on mathematics in 1923 and subsequently published almost nothing. In fact, he retracted some of the little that he had written. His book *Philosophical Investigations* was published in 1953 after his death. So what did he do that caused his fellow philosophers to rank him up there with Plato and Aristotle? It seems that the great philosophers are the ones who keep asking "what do you mean by that?" over and over again until you want to throttle them. Like Kant and Nietzsche and Socrates, Wittgenstein knocked the props from under both revealed religion and scientific philosophy and made practitioners in multiple fields rethink how they were doing business.

Let's look more closely at his technique, because Wittgenstein is a process philosopher, meaning that the way he does philosophy is to pry back the layers on the words used to continually refine what that word means in its actual context. The process (what he calls word games) is laborious and sometimes obscure and at the end of it all, one should be sure of the answer, but often is not.

Meaning is use. That is the slogan that epitomizes but doesn't come close to explaining Wittgenstein's approach. For him, understanding is not necessarily a mental process, but rather a circumstance through which we suddenly say "now I get it." We do this by experience, by discussing with others, by making connections and above all, by understanding the context in which we use particular words. It is a mental chess game, but it is not inward looking like Descartes' *Cogito, ergo sum*. It requires forgetting all the outward rules of philosophy and just messing with the words we use.

One example of a word game that goes on and on is his question of how we know about pain. Can we know it without experiencing it? How do we describe it? Could we teach a dog to simulate (fake) pain? Is a dog too honest? Does the concept of pain depend on the language we have learned? The point is not to be silly (although some of the questions might suggest that) but to teach clear thinking, to strip away all of the undefined terms, all of the extraneous assumptions, all of the unexamined premises. Once this is done, the traditional philosophical problems dissolve.

Rowton

No, Wittgenstein says they dissolve. For me, all the problems are still there and on top of it I have to read all this endless stuff that makes no sense. I am going to give you my take on Wittgenstein and on academics in general: you make your mark with your colleagues by being so obscure that none of them dare call your bluff because they don't want to look stupid.

Deconstructing words may be the end of the issue for Wittgenstein, but the rest of the philosophical world still wanted to wrestle with the nature of God, arguing about what is moral, what is right, true, and just. That Wittgenstein would have none of it forced virtually everyone else to rethink how they were thinking. It is the philosophers who upset the apple cart—who give their fellows a swift kick in the pants—that make history.

Carol Gilligan, who is labeled more as a psychologist and behavioralist than a philosopher, has had an enormous impact on medical ethics by suggesting that the patient should have a say in what happens rather than the doctor just making the call. Females, she argues, have gotten short shrift in a male dominated system that depends on exposition of rights and rules. Women are more attuned to relationships and caring. Women listen. Often men don't.

She reminds us of Wittgenstein because she says that the way people talk about their lives matters, both in the language they use and in the context and connections they make. So she asks four questions about women's voices: who is speaking, in what body, telling what story, and in what cultural framework. But while Wittgenstein was perfectly willing to call almost anybody an idiot, Gilligan says women are much more hesitant to judge because they appreciate the complexity of relationships.

ROWTON

You can judge without being judgmental. Like: "That was a really crappy performance, but I am not saying you are a bad person." But I groove on Gilligan's point: there shouldn't be a single mode of experience for interpreting the human condition. Men view the world through an ethic of justice where everyone should be treated the same; women rely on an ethic of care that rests on a premise of nonviolence where no one should be hurt. If that is not what she means, blame me. Yah, yah, not all women think the same and not all men are dorks.

A WORD ABOUT THINKING

One could divide the world in simplifiers and complicators. The complicator has to make every piece of the puzzle fit, and as a consequence, the thought process has lots of twigs and branches to accommodate all of the salient facts and all of the asides and explanations on the route to a conclusion. A simplifier's tree is straight and narrow—the only facts that matter are the ones absolutely necessary for the conclusion.

Likewise, there are linear and nebular thinkers. The linear thinker proceeds from point *a* to point *b* and concludes, inexorably, that the answer is *c*. The nebular thinker considers everything that flashes through the mind because no thought is irrelevant to the process of information gathering that, at some random point, will spit out a conclusion.

Probably most of us fit into each of these categories at one time or another, but I suspect our brains are wired to favor one method over another. As a trial lawyer, I have seen both clear thinking and consummate stupidity prove successful on a jury of our peers. The brilliant arguments were not always the winning ones.

About the last person one would expect to be a champion for certainty of thought is Wittgenstein. Others in his philosophical realm such as Bertrand Russell called certainty "intellectual vice." What Wittgenstein said is that if we want to make our way through life, we have to start somewhere. "At the foundation of a well-founded belief lies belief that is not founded." Since we have to start somewhere, why not believe that the sun is going to rise in the east or that the Cubs will win the series or that there is a God?

Rowers snuggle up to Wittgenstein. Why not believe you are going to win and then base all of your rational preparation on that assumption? It is just common sense, he would argue, because if you start with the belief that you can't or won't win, you have no chance and you probably won't even try.

CHAPTER 27

Religion

"The good life is one inspired by love and guided by reason." Bertrand Russell

You may have noticed that God has a certain resiliency despite the various philosophers such as Nietzsche and Sartre who have declared Him obsolete. Religion is a touchy subject, particularly since I am about to tell you that mine ended up in the dumpster somewhere along life's highway. But this does tie in with rowing, believe it or not, and I am about to tell you how.

Mine was a church family fueled by my mother's faith, and as I grew up we went to Sunday school, vacation bible school, youth fellowship, services, sermons, and prayer groups. We sang in every imaginable choral group, but we never seemed to get Sunday organized enough to get to church on time. So we sat in the back.

My two brothers, sister, and I all studied music and had trained voices, and when we cut loose on the second hymn (we missed the first one), we would count the number of turn-arounds we got. That was the most fun part of the sometimes interminable service.

Perhaps there is a religion gene that makes one susceptible to faith. Recent neuroscience suggests as much. I was receptive enough to want to give religion a thorough look so I went to Union Theological Seminary in New York after I graduated from college. I was waiting for the KA-BOOM, Saul on the road to Damascus, moment where God announced that I was His guy. Didn't happen.

So I muddled along, took a master's degree in ethics and went to law school. Theology was not compelling because it depends on persuasion alone while the law has teeth—money judgments or jail. As that great humanitarian Al Capone put it: "you can get farther with a kind word and a gun than a kind word alone."

What I learned in two years of theological studies served me well for the next couple of decades. We took our boys to church. They hated it. We went less and less and then not at all.

Finally I admitted to myself that religion played almost no part in my life and that I believed in neither salvation nor damnation. The focus of popular religion on personal salvation and afterlife seemed to me to be both selfish and an excuse for not confronting the problems caused by the flawed and irrational creatures who are our fellow human beings.

Moreover, a 2,000-year-old world view, as expressed in the Bible, while not without its wisdom, just carried too much baggage and required a suspension of disbelief I was no longer able to embrace.

But that is not the end of the story. Part of my divorce from religion is due to sweet old—101 years when we met her—Margaret Redman. The choir of the First Presbyterian Church migrated down to sit among and sing hymns with the vocally challenged congregation. One Sunday Leah and I sat next to this little lady with the pill box hat who turned out to be a dynamo.

She had climbed all the Northwest Cascade volcanoes multiple times, skied before there were lifts, and still lived in her own house where she cooked, cleaned, gardened, and read Shakespeare. It was Margaret who gave us permission to miss church. "I always got my renewal by being outside with nature," she said. "Climb a mountain and you will know God." So we went skiing with our boys on the weekends and of the dozen best conversations I had with each of them as they were growing up, three-quarters took place on the ski lift.

So, is there a hole in my life where religion used to be? There is a universal longing for inclusion and for the comfort that we are not alone, adrift in a hostile universe. But relax, I am not going to declare Rowology a religion. I do think, however, that roasting one's brain with sweat, moving the boat through the water, and pushing one's physical limits releases some of the endorphins that cause a feeling of well-being similar to the religious experience.

The mind/body dichotomy of Plato and others is one I categorically reject. We clarify our minds by exercising our bodies. Ask anyone who has suffered from depression and she will tell you the best way to blast that debilitating black dog out of your head is with exercise.

Granted, rowing is not like a systematic theology that will help you put the blocks of the universe in place. Rowology doesn't have a god-head or a good book or incense, bells or cathedrals. But it does clear away the mental rubble and by so doing makes my mind more receptive to spirituality.

Extreme experiences tend to clear away the detritus of daily life. Antarctic explorer Ernest Shackleton, whose ordeal defined the word extreme, spoke of "piercing the veneer of outside things and hearing the text that nature renders to reach the naked soul of man." While I don't recommend 800 miles across Antarctic seas in an open boat, pushing yourself to your physical limits may open some spiritual portals.

Rowing also provides the community of like-minded companions to which one can belong. The rowing community is one of the most open and accepting of any I have known.

Think of rowing, then, as a primer for spirituality. Think of it as sandpaper, as solvent, as a dozer blade, as a mind rake. Rowing doesn't provide the substance of belief, but it does lay fertile the pasture, unlock the mind, and stimulate the imagination. And that is worth a lot.

The will to believe is a vital and undeniable human force. Einstein put it best by saying that the most beautiful thing we can experience is the mysterious—the knowledge of the existence of something unfathomable to us. To him, this awe was the basis for religiosity. The most important function of art and science is to awaken and keep alive the spirit of inquisitive wonder.

Helen Keller took the thought one step further away from organized religion by espousing a faith completely cut free from creed or dogma. She described an active faith that knows no fear, but operates with a dignity that is a worthy companion to the beautiful, the good and the true.

The answer to each seeker will be different. But man is a seeker and so religion must and will be an influence on all of our lives.

Chapter 28

Opening Day

"Practice puts brains in your muscles." Sam Snead

It's a three day party. Seattle is a boat town and everybody who floats or paddles or sails or even thinks about the water is out there on the first weekend in May to welcome in the new season. It's noisy and exuberant and marinated in lots of alcohol—from Friday afternoon to some time on Sunday when the revelers begin to remember they have to go to work on Monday.

The rowing regatta is incidental to most of the revelers, but is a prize invitation to those who are called upon to participate. The course is 2,000 meters and only four boats are in each race because that is how many can fit abreast through the Montlake cut that connects lakes Washington and Union. To mark the course, log booms extend from the start line to the cut and nested, stern in, are the boats of the revelers. Here is a guy in a king Tut headdress. There a boat named *Off Piste*. A baby blue amphacar trailing a jolly roger flag in the water putts by looking as if a small wave could fill it like a bathtub.

The royalty of Opening Day is there in their resplendent white trousers, navy blue jackets, shoulder boards with fringe and three cornered "trilby" hats. Lots of dogs—full time barkers. Ship's bells, whistles and, at the end of the course, the University of Washington band with the tubas twirling around as they play. This is a PARTY.

We launch from the University of Washington's Taj Mahal of a boathouse, and in the warm up area is a floating crane sporting the biggest of American flags. Next to it is a fire boat with water cannons shooting out huge streams of water in festive disregard of the prevailing wind that blows the spray across our already rain drenched and bedraggled uniforms.

The race has no stake boats to hold us in place and the starters do their best to get alignment in a persistent cross wind. "Corvallis, you are supposed to take your clothes off in the warm up area," he says as our bow person madly tries to get her sweat shirt off before we start. One stroke and we crash into the boat on our port. Somebody yells "keep rowing," and we shoot across two lanes and crash into the two boats on our starboard, and then we break free and we are off. For

750 meters we are neck and neck with the Ancient Mariners and then we pull away, and through the cut we can hear the cheers and the dogs and the horns and bells and even someone calling our names. We cross the line first, but don't know if we are disqualified for the kung fu start.

The best part of the race is yet to come, though. All of the boats in all of the races have to wait until the last race is done because the cut is too narrow for boats to be going both ways. Then all of the boats process back through the cut and along the log booms and all the way the spectators are clapping and yelling thanks for participating and it is truly grand.

We drove back to Corvallis after the race, all except for Bob and Susan, who stayed for the medal presentation where we would either get some hardware or a kick in the pants. Bob called as we were just about home and the whole car erupted when he said he had a handful of medals. Nice ones too, with porcelain and what is, no doubt, real gold, and a nice picture of the Seattle Yacht Club.

Philosophical Insight

It strikes me that there is nothing false about rowing. The water tells you how it likes your stroke. Too deep and the boat rocks; too shallow and it splashes at the release. The boat moves only as you direct it, and the time clocked at the end of the race is what you did. No baloney.

Not much in life is that honest. Even when we are trying to recall an event, as an eye witness to an auto accident, for example, our brains fill in details and as we rehearse what happened, we make the story fit our mental picture. As a lifelong trial lawyer, I can tell you that that picture is often wrong. Not wrong out of malice, but wrong out of the very human need to make sense of things.

A drill we often do in practice is to row with our eyes closed. This lets you "feel" the stroke and listen for the clunk as the oar squares up against the pin, and sense the swing of the other rowers as their bodies move out of bow toward the stern in preparation for the catch. This is rowing in a state of grace. It is singular and total and unadulterated without any outside influence, and at that moment the totality of the world is one with your body and the boat and the water.

There is a communal binder in such an experience. You become one with your fellow rowers. You think, "I can count on this person." You think, "we know the same stuff, can do the same things, have been through the same experiences." What does it mean to be reliable and to be relied on? It is the glue that makes friendships and communities and fighting forces and nations. It is the indispensable element of any society, any group, any successful adventure. It is why soldiers who have fought together remain buddies for life. To be reliable and relied on is wonderful and noble and moral.

CHAPTER 29

Martin Luther King, Jr. (1929–1968) and Michael Walzer (1935–)

"The time is always right to do the right thing." Martin Luther King, Jr.

We in the United States are not, as a culture, philosophical types. We don't sit around contemplating—we get things done. We produce, we consume, we drive fast and we swagger. It isn't that we don't have thinkers; it is just that we, as a society, often seem too busy to think. So we keep doing the same stuff, much of it destructive—to the environment, to our social fabric, to our own self-interest.

Yet choices are made, even if the choice is a non-choice—deciding not to decide. Martin Luther King, Jr., writing from the Birmingham jail, articulates the philosophical case for justice and action with a clarity and passion that ranks him among the most compelling of American philosophers. He is writing to a group of fellow clergy, Christian and Jewish, and is responding to their criticism that he is moving too fast and may lose the support of those who want gradual change in race relations. Those who oppress never relinquish that power voluntarily, he says, and justice delayed is justice denied.

One can break the law if the law is unjust. An unjust law doesn't conform to the law of God and accepted morality. It degrades human personality. It is imposed on the minority by the majority; it is passed when Negroes are prevented from voting; it is applied unequally. One who breaks an unjust law must do so openly, lovingly and with a willingness to accept the penalty. That is why he is in jail, and that is why his correspondents should get off their comfortable back sides and get him out. To disobey an unjust law, he says, shows the greatest respect for the law.

Moderation in the face of injustice is immoral. Nothing will change without rubbing raw the sores of discontent (not his phrase, but that of Saul Alinsky). Violence may happen, but one cannot blame the peaceful protester any more than one can blame the victim of robbery for having money. Time is neutral and time alone will not overcome the "appalling silence of the good people." He says he is an extremist in the same sense as Jesus and Martin Luther and Thomas Jefferson, but he stands between the entreaties for violence by the angriest Negroes and

110

those who have been so dehumanized as to accept segregation. He quotes John Bunyan: "I will stay in jail until the end of my days before I make a butchery of my conscience."

Most of us have studied philosophy because we have read the *Letter from Birmingham Jail* in school. It contains an issue, an argument, and a justification. The best of philosophy makes us think. Political philosophy such as this should move us to action. Philosophy, after all, deals with the most serious and important issues of our lives. Words do have power.

More American Philosophy

After what I have said about how philosophical we aren't, perhaps you expect this to be a short list, but philosophy has been popping up all over in the latter part of the twentieth century. Ethnic studies, gender studies, queer studies, educational philosophy, the resurgence of the ever popular God, inter-cultural philosophy, theories of knowledge, arguments about whether we have free will or are determined by some preprogrammed force are all thrashing about in the minds and on the computers of lots of people, probably even that person sitting next to you.

I will venture into this thicket only to give one example, that being Michael Walzer's argument of why he wants a politician to have "dirty hands." He starts out with the proposition that we all hustle, lie, and fudge to get what we want. This is consistent with the Christian theological position that we are all sinners. The rub comes then, when the elected official is expected to lie, cheat and hustle *for us*. He or she can't help serving her own self-interest because you are a lousy (and unsuccessful) politician if you don't want power, don't want to get elected, and once elected, don't want to stay there.

But what if we elect a politician because we think her of high moral standards? Can she serve without getting her hands dirty? Of course not. It is a dirty process. As the playwright Anton Chekhov put it: "one does not put on his best trousers when he goes out to fight for truth and justice." So what do we think if our candidate makes a deal with a crooked ward boss to get elected? Walzer's answer? She should do it because we want her to, but she should feel guilty. The guilty conscience is the equivalent of dirty hands and that is the best we can expect.

What do you think? I would be disappointed if you, by now, didn't want to rip a few logical layers off of this argument and see what remains. I would be equally disappointed if you didn't think it would be fun to do so.

Rowton

He didn't ask me what I think. Walzer's concern is what the politician does once he or she is elected, not what the politician does to get elected. What's more, Walzer is calling for a public ritual of penance so a leader with dirty hands can seek public forgiveness (which is consistent with both what Camus and Martin Luther King, Jr. write). The point is to make public morality public so that citizens don't become disengaged and cynical.

CHAPTER 30

Chauvinistic, Sexist, Misanthropic Bastards

> "At the heart of liberty is the right to define one's own concept of existence, of the meaning of the universe, and of the mystery of human life." David Souter, Supreme Court Justice

While there are physical differences between the sexes, the size of the brain and ability to think aren't among them. So why is it that when recounting the history of philosophy, women thinkers are at best a footnote? Let me venture a few reasons before concluding, as the title of this chapter not so subtly suggests, that the history of philosophy is as sexist and self-satisfied as the leather chairs in the smoking room of the Downtown Testosterone Club.

The Bible is one. Subjugation of women to their husbands, the expectation of female obedience, the male making all of the decisions—all of those positions can be derived from the Bible. But a fair reading can also produce an ethic of equality, of love, and of caretaking. By analogy, the Bible can be the justification for conquering the earth, getting rich, and claiming wealth is a sign of God's favor (John Calvin, for example) or it can be read as requiring us to be stewards of God's creation and care for the earth and all of it creatures (a theory that has come to the table only lately, and perhaps far too late to undo the devastation of the pillaging theory).

A second historical reason is that, because they are the nurturers, women have been confined to the home, at least until the infant is self-sufficient, and for humans, that is an extraordinarily long time. Our baby goats are off on their own in a couple of months. Late teens is when we declare a human to be self-sufficient, at least in a legal sense, and neuro-science tells us that the brain is not fully mature until the mid-twenties.

ROWTON

Tell us something we don't know.

There are dozens more theories for male privilege, none of which serve as justification, but the fact remains that the history of philosophy has been written by males, about males and for males. A few of those males at least gave lip service to the other gender. Plato touched on it in his politics saying that the guardians—those who were fit to rule—could be of either gender. J. S. Mill wrote a book titled *The Subjugation of Women* that to this day is a clarion call for equal rights and equal treatment. Kant defined the social contract as an agreement among people of freedom and equality, but he didn't really champion the cause of women. And then there is Nietzsche who was about as sexist and misogynistic as they come.

Philosophy discovered women in the second half of the twentieth century. While men were off killing each other in World War II, Philippa Foot was writing some fine philosophy in Great Britain. I have mentioned the work of Carol Gilligan, who in the early 1980s emphasized caring and involvement of the individual over rules and regulations in ethical theory. Others such as Annette Baier focused on relationships of trust, using the model of infant and mother. Rather than an ethics of obligation, some feminine writers emphasized an ethics of love, recognizing than none of us is self-sufficient and all of us exist in a community that is bound by something more than a set of rules.

Another dimension of ethics holds, as is found in the writings of Alison Jaggar, that subordination of women, regardless of its reason, is ethically wrong and women are entitled to the same treatment, the same respect, as men. This ethics is focused on power, and instead of the blind justice model of the American legal system, writers such as Mary Daly invoke the goddess Nemesis, whose eyes are wide open, all three of them. Nemesis is about helping the oppressed more than punishing the guilty in this philosophical system. The Nemesis of mythology is appropriately female, but as the "daughter of justice," she was one tough lady. Known as one from whom escape was impossible, she brought divine retribution to all who were arrogant. She is, no doubt, still very busy.

Sarah Lucia Hoagland writes that a new approach to ethics is not to get back at men and give them the same kind of subservient status under which females suffered for millennia, but to assure that the most vulnerable and the least secure of our society have the ability to make choices and direct their own existence. Even when the oppressed cannot control a situation, at least they can influence it. Power here is about the sanctity of choice and, she adds, we must not discount playfulness, which I take to mean that life is to be celebrated and enjoyed.

This by no means is meant to be a survey of feminine or feminist writers, but merely an acknowledgement that philosophy is no longer the sole property of males, and we are all the better for it. Usually the law follows ethics in the sense that the moral outrage over injustice such as slavery, child labor or segregation leads to legislation like the 13th, 14th, and 15th Amendments and cases such as

Brown v. Board of Education (declaring separate but equal schools were inherently unequal). My sense, which I would be hard pressed to defend if I had to, is that the law has lead morality in gender issues. Legislation such as sex discrimination laws, particularly in the work place, have had a significant role in opening a lot of male eyes to the fact that women are perfectly capable of deep thinking. There remain, however, many male heads that are filled with sawdust.

Rowing, I am pleased to say, is an equal opportunity sport in every sense. Much of this is due to Title IX, the Federal Law that mandates equality of resources and opportunity in college athletics. I am aware of one school that has seventeen scholarships in rowing for women and none for men. Of course, that hardly makes up for the overwhelming presence of football, but it is a step in the right direction.

Collegiate and masters competitions are gender neutral, although separate but equal does apply and works fairly here. What I mean is that the women don't have to race against the men. In masters, though, lots of races are for mixed boats. One time we had a men's four race without enough men, so one of our women "manned-up" and we had a dandy race. She still remembers it as one of her favorites.

CHAPTER 31

Jurisprudence

"Never trust a rabbit to deliver the lettuce. Probably a maxim of equity."

The philosophy of law, is not just for those afflicted with legalitis as a profession. It seeks, at least in part, to make a distinction between what we ask of the law and what is left to morality.

The law says you can or you can't and if you do or you don't we will put you in jail or fine you. Morality says, you should or shouldn't and if you do or don't, society may shun you, or some superior being may judge you, but you have a choice. Where the law gets into trouble is when legislatures try to impose morality through the law. Examples: school prayer, abortion, gay marriage, contraception. The law depends for its force upon wide acceptance so that most people voluntarily obey. When that is missing, it weakens the social structure because respect for the law is essential to democracy. Examples of laws not widely accepted: fifty-five-mile-per-hour speed limit and prohibition.

Significant issues in jurisprudence include the death penalty, mandatory prison sentences, cruel and unusual punishment (like water boarding), where the criminal law should apply and when, if ever, military law should apply (if terrorism or insurrection is an issue), the role of money in politics, and who gets to have lethal weapons. Affirmative action is another hot one, as are the boundaries of sex, age, disability, and every other kind of discrimination, and who should get to live here and be a citizen and whether health care is a right or a privilege and who pays for it.

Jurisprudence also tackles such thorny issues as whether retribution or rehabilitation is best for criminals, whether the power to tax is the power to destroy, whether money and voting are the same thing, the balance between first amendment speech and 14th amendment equal protection, and the beat goes on. The nose of jurisprudence is in everyone's tent because the law is everywhere. And while judges are bound by *stare decisis*, the legal rule that requires them to follow prior opinions, jurisprudence has the luxury of pondering what the law should be. There is plenty of room for improvement.

Rowton

Is that it? Even in a book of acknowledged superficiality, is he just going to throw out a laundry list of community splitting issues and call it good?

In a word, yes. Sorry.

Philosophy generally doesn't have a hierarchy. If you are Socrates or even Nietzsche, you can try to persuade your fellow philosophers you are right about most things, that your brain and your ego are superior and that a school ought to be named after you. The law is different. An appellate court can reverse a lower court, and the Supreme Court of the United States is the final arbiter of what Federal law and the United States Constitution mean. Lower courts are bound thereby.

Final means that a particular challenge is settled. But final doesn't mean final forever. In the thorny and unfortunate history of slavery in the United States, slaves were at one time declared to be property. Then, during the Civil War, they were freed and given equal protection by constitutional Amendment. Then courts held that "separate but equal" schools were constitutional. Then they weren't.

Just because the Supreme Court is the final word doesn't mean its justices are any less human or any less prone to human error. That is why Jurisprudence, the philosophy of law, is so important. It serves as a vital check on the power of the courts and the evolution of the law. While Wittgenstein's game theory may not much influence our daily lives, the law is everywhere, every day.

More Entertainment for Philosophers

We have talked about Occam's razor (cut out the BS and get to the point), and Plato's cave (we talked about that, didn't we?) If not, Plato's cave has folks who can't move so they can see only their shadows cast on the wall by firelight. This is a metaphor for the imperfect way we perceive the world. By exploring the world of ideas, we can train our minds to know the perfect form—say the perfect baseball bat or the perfect baloney sandwich (perhaps not a good example).

Anyway, a couple more mind games that entertain philosophers are Buridan's ass and Pascal's wager. Buridan's ass relates to free will in humankind and the example is a donkey between two tasty stacks of hay who can't decide which delectable one to eat and so starves to death. The point is that man must choose and it is his reason that helps him find the greater good. Moderns are more likely to say that the two hay stacks are really two equally stinky bad choices and we have to do the best we can.

Pascal's wager is the bet that there is an afterlife. He is going with the odds like a good gambler, reasoning that your life is finite but paradise is forever so why not play the smart money and bet on afterlife. What have you got to lose? The small problem is that this is a tad cynical, because at least in Christianity, you are saved by faith, not by a clever wager. But hey, if it entertains the philosophers, carry on.

Then there is trolley-ology. It comes from English philosopher Philippa Foot (1920–2010) who posed the moral dilemma of an out of control trolley hurtling down the track and dead ahead are five people who cannot get out of the way. The conductor can divert to a spur where only one person will be killed. What to do? Other ethicists added their gloss: a person standing by the track can throw the switch; the conductor is unconscious, should a passenger make this life and death decision? Is it alright to throw a fat man off the bridge to stop the car? Is it ethical to do nothing?

Of special interest to rowers, who row because it is fun, is the play theory of Friedrich Schiller (d. 1805). He argued that by play we discover our own self-consciousness, our freedom and hence our morality. "Man plays only when he is in the full sense of the word a man, and he is only wholly a Man when he is playing." He wrote that in *On the Aesthetic Education of Man* in 1795. He also wrote *Ode to Joy* which became the words to the last movement of Beethoven's Ninth symphony proclaiming the freedom and brotherhood of man. The theory is cogent because much of what we learn about life, we learn by playing as children. Why should we stop playing, and learning, just because we are adults? Indeed, why should we grow up?

CHAPTER 32

Sex, Rowing, and Philosophy

> "Mankind. It's made up of two words. Mank and ind. What does that mean?" Jack Handy, *Saturday Night Live*

With philosophy, particularly if the discipline is defined as "action guided by reflection," it is hard to see how sex wouldn't be a major topic of discussion. That is not the case with most philosophers. Yes, some, like St. Augustine had rakish youths, but most write as if sex doesn't play a major role in the motivations of human kind. It does. It causes us to do stupid things. It starts wars, provokes murders, rends communities. Moreover, sexual encounters lead to issues of rejection, of constancy, of love, happiness, or despair. Those are the stock and trade of philosophy, so how come sex isn't front and center?

Perhaps the answer lies in the difference between sex and love. Sex satisfies, at least for a few minutes, the animal urge that keeps the species from perishing. I can only speak for the male gender, but the statistic of thinking about sex every twelve minutes in males is not far off the mark. This is raw impulse, not born of rational reflection.

But what can be said of love, then? Is it not also irrational? Can saying: "I love thee, let me count the ways" actually capture the essence of love? To say I love you because you are [and here insert five or fifty traits] foretells a train wreck in a relationship because the minute the person changes, or stops doing or modifies those traits, the relationship is in trouble. Love is made of sterner stuff and, like so much that is essentially spiritual, is indefinable. I can define what people who are in love do, like appreciate each other, do things for each other, talk to each other, have sex with each other, but the sum total of these actions leaves us far short of a meaningful definition of love. And perhaps that is why it is the poets and singers, not the philosophers, who embrace the ethereal nature of love.

By now you know that I am not a fan of St. Paul, but his description of love in 1 Corinthians 13 is one of the best and most lyrical. Paraphrasing, he says even if I am silver-tongued, prophetic, cloaked with faith and deliver my body to be burned I am nothing without love. It is a remarkable statement because he elevates love over faith. Then he wades into the deep waters of defining love: "Love is patient and kind; love is not jealous or boastful; it is not arrogant or rude. Love does not insist on its own way; it is not irritable or resentful; it does not rejoice at wrong, but rejoices in the right. Love bears all things, believes all things, hopes all things, endures all things."

He is talking about *agape* not eros love so the description of what love does is more applicable to communities or friendships than couples. And while I have no quarrel with love not being arrogant or boastful or any of the other negative characteristics he lists, couples love—eros—can be all of those things and still endure and prosper as long as there is a way to get the relationship grounded again. In a book the title of which I will not mention to protect the guilty, the revolting phrase used over and over is: "Love means never having to say you're sorry." What a crock. One thing about love I know for sure is that if you love somebody you better be ready to say "I'm sorry" early and often. We all make mistakes, do mean things, are thoughtless and selfish, and we hurt the ones we love. Just listen to the lyrics of any country song. Love prevails when we swallow pride, suck it up, and humble ourselves before the one we love, not because we have to but because we want to make it right.

While St. Paul and I may be talking about different kinds of love, on this we agree: love is the most important impulse and commitment of humankind.

A kind of love that classical philosophy highly valued and modern philosophy pretty much ignores is friendship. If everything is classified in sexual terms, such as straight or LGBTQ, or whatever unacknowledged category comes to society's attention, then the discussion tends to be about rights and discrimination or makeups and breakups. Friendship, on the other hand, is about trust and companionship, and fellowship and appreciation. It is here that rowing excels. Teamwork and mutual dependence are the key. No rower can lift a multiple person shell alone—it has to be done together and in rhythm or the boat will be damaged. Every rower in the boat is responsible to everyone else. The glory is collective. The work is shared. The mutual admiration, contagious.

Humans have a universal longing for inclusion. We identify, in part, by our family, our geographical community, and our nation.

Rowing clubs and teams celebrate birthdays, individual achievements at work, successes and near misses at regattas, and the pure pleasure of being together—hanging out in the tent between races and just talking, eating power bars and feeling good. Friendship is comfortable. It is love of others expressed in hugs rather than sexual possession. This kind of friendship creates multiple bonds and there is great health in it. Friendship, at its root, is about others, not about you.

I don't mean to suggest here that philosophers have not written about love. Plato's dialogue entitled *Symposium* is a narrative of various men lying around a room on couches, each giving an oration about the nature of love. Early on Socrates says that love is the only thing he knows about. But as usual in Socratic dialogues, we come away with more questions than answers. That is the point. Plato wants to draw us into the discussion to articulate and then defend our position.

Here is one example, a speech given by Agathon who faults his fellow revelers for focusing on what the god love can do for humans rather that the characteristics of the god himself. Compare with St. Paul's description above: "[H]e provides gentleness and banishes savagery; he loves to give good will, hates to give ill will; gracious; mild; illustrious to the wise;...careful of good things; enviable to those who have none of him, treasured by those who have some of him."

Much of what Plato writes about Socrates is to refute the Sophists who look to human experience to explain all that happens. To them, reality is in flux—they are, in short, relativists. Plato is for absolutes. There is a perfect form and it is by that form that we recognize what something really is. In Plato's case, the form of love in its purest sense is in the mind—the equivalent of philosophy. Thus he bitches out the poets (whom he would ban from the ideal state) because they mess with language, embrace flux and destabilize the just city. And, their love is of the boy, girl variety.

ROWTON

Congratulations, big boy, you have finally discovered one of the eternal philosophical schisms: between those like the Sophists and Nietzsche who want to destabilize language and embrace uncertainty, and those like Plato who want form, definiteness and stability.

I haven't said nearly enough about sex here. Western philosophers have their shorts in a bunch about sex, but not so those of the non-Western world. So what I suggest is that if you want to learn a few new moves or different positions, read the *Kama Sutra*.

CHAPTER 33

Choking

> "To discover reality, the only person you have to convince is yourself." Anon.

Choking. What an awful, hateful ego-erasing disaster. We all know it—performing at less than our best—sometimes miles below expectations. It is, my friends, a case of our minds mugging our bodies. Not all of our corpuscles are on the same team.

We practice to develop muscle memory so that every stroke is the same as the one before, and the one after, into eternity and forevermore, amen. Arms away, body over, slow slide, quick catch, leg drive, body layback, finish high, quick turn around and do it again. We are like a machine: precise, powerful, unflappable. Until the big race.

Picture it. You and your teammates won all the dual meets, the regionals and now you are in the finals of THE BIG ONE. Your coach, bless him, says: "Think of what this means, men." And thereby, he gives you the worst advice possible because when it comes to THE BIG ONE, thinking is the last thing you want to do. You want to stay loose, get a good night's sleep and let your body do what it is so superbly conditioned to do. The quasi-philosophical term is sprezzatura: effortless grace.

If you dwell on "what this means" you are screwed. The pre-frontal cortex of your brain is where the shoot-me-in-the-foot thinking comes from. You start deconstructing your stroke, thinking about your hands, or your oar depth or that little tweak in your back and the result is uniformly shitty. You do less than your best because your brain has tripped over your muscles.

In a book about philosophy, admonishing you not to think is admittedly paradoxical, but perhaps this is one instance in which Plato's mind-body separation makes sense. Your body knows what to do because of the hours and hours of practice. Leave the mind home. You can do without it for 2,000 meters. We have talked about Flow—the kind of out-of-body experience where everything clicks and the results are beyond marvelous. It really is an in-body and out-of-mind experience and that is why we seldom can remember the details of the perfect race, the stunning aria, the soaring high jump. The folks who study this stuff call it "procedural memory."

In a moment of ego shattering confession, let me say that I have choked—as I suspect most of us have at one time or another. The sports choke I remember most vividly was on hole number 8 in a Medford High golf match against Marshfield. Paul Evanson was our coach and happened to be walking with me as I hit a mid iron to within three feet of the cup. Paul was ecstatic. "Now we've got 'em" he chortled. I stood over the putt, my incompletely formed but over active pre-frontal cortex yelling, "don't ram it" and three putted from three feet. Choke-city.

In singing, choking may be even more pervasive, invasive and insidious than in sports. Singing (not the Love Me Tender kind of crooning, but the guts ball Mozart aria or Handel oratorio) requires constant breath support that is honed by decades of practice. You breathe from your diaphragm (look at an opera singer's shoulders; they never move when they breath), the air flows up with support as if you were sitting on a saddle, resonates in the nasal cavities and flows out your mouth, round and elegant, forming the words with perfect diction in any one of a dozen languages.

I have seen and heard beautifully trained singers choke and everyone—the audience and the performer—feels terrible about it. The question, really, is why? Why do we do so poorly when we should do so well? Why do we practice like champs and perform like goobers?

One answer is that we do *not* practice as if we were performing. If we practice as if we were on stage or in the race, we improve our chances with focus and intensity, but even that is no guarantee. We need a strategy to keep the genie in the box—to keep our minds from sticking in—to keep the pre-frontal cortex in the back seat.

Meditation helps some. I like to sing a song in my mind to keep the "don't hit it in the ditch" gremlins away. Breathing exercises help. I have imagined drawing a curtain on a stage to block out the negative images. The trick is to distract yourself in the internecine struggle pitting one part of your body against another. But it is why, intentionally or not, NIKE's slogan "Just do it" is exactly right.

By the way, Dan Wieden of Wieden+Kennedy, the extraordinary marketers who developed that slogan, says it came to him when he was thinking about a Florida serial killer who was telling his executioners to turn on the juice. The mind is an unruly and thoroughly unpredictable beast.

Anyway, "just do it" is so appropriate for athletes and performers because you have trained your fanny off and there is nothing left but to go out there to the track, the pool, the race course or the stage and JUST DO IT. And if you take your mind along, god help you.

You may wonder why little kids, particularly in gymnastics, but increasingly in all sports, are drubbing their adult competitors. One answer is that the pre-frontal cortex is not fully developed until we are about twenty-five years old, so kids have less of a Jekyll and Hyde dialogue going on in their skulls. Another is that the older we get the more experiences we have chalked up, and those all weigh in on how we react to stress. For some, the adrenaline rush is a call to perform and for others, an alarm to freeze.

My final word on this subject, coming in part from the heart and in part from the brain, is that in the event you are in a performance situation, say sitting at the starting line, in lane number 5, at the Nationals, and you find that your head has come along, don't panic, just think "smooth." Smooth. Smooth seems to work for damn near everything.

CHAPTER 34

Viktor Frankl (1905–1997)

"That which doesn't kill me, makes me stronger." Nietzsche

I'm sitting here looking at the raw skin on the thumb of my feathering hand after the first hard, on-water row of the season and feeling the pain. Pain and suffering are part of the sport of rowing, and they are willfully encountered, embraced even, because they have meaning. That meaning is that if you want to be good, if you want to win, pain is part of the equation. Compared to the pain suffered by Viktor Frankl, however, the pain of rowing is about as significant as the blister on my thumb.

Frankl is not usually grouped with modern philosophers since his field was psychology, but his insights, forged in the horrors of Auschwitz and Dachau, give his writing an authenticity that ranks his book, *Man's Search for Meaning*, among the most important of the twentieth century. He observes that one's chance of living through a Nazi concentration camp was no better than one in twenty-eight. Survival was a matter of whim—a finger raised, an order to go to the right, not the left, a stumble on a work crew, locking eyes with a feckless guard. A trip to the showers could mean a delousing or death by poison gas. Beatings were routine; hunger and disease ever-present.

Frankl could have used the visa he was granted in 1941 to leave Austria and come to America, but felt he could not abandon his parents who would inevitably be sent to the camps. He could have escaped the camps toward the end of the war, but chose to stay and continue to treat his fellow prisoners there. Few can speak with more authority about the nature of suffering. Surprisingly, he concludes that suffering has meaning: it matters not what we expect from life—we must concentrate on what life expects of us.

He quotes Spinoza in saying that suffering ceases to be suffering as soon as we form a clear and precise picture of it. No one can relieve man of his suffering or suffer in his place. Man's unique opportunity lies in the way he bears his burden. Frankl's conclusion, formed by observing those that survived and those that perished, is that the survivors focused on something that had meaning beyond themselves—something in the future to which they were committed.

He gives two examples of men who were in despair and suicidal. On interrogating the first, he found that he had a child who was safe in a foreign country and awaiting his father to return to him. A second man had left a scientific manuscript unfinished before the war. In both cases, the men realized they had something for which to live. According to Frankl, striving to find meaning is the primary motivational force for humans. Mental health is based on a tension between what we have already achieved and what we can and should become in the future. Thus the essence of human existence is responsibility. Live as if you were living your life for the second time and have an opportunity to do better.

Happiness is not a goal, but something that is a byproduct of a meaningful existence, and a meaningful existence, in turn, can be gained in three ways: through experience, though love, or through overcoming suffering. If life has meaning, then suffering has to have meaning as well.

Frankl doesn't present a systematic philosophy as much as an attitude toward health. He had plenty of cause for bitterness or despair (his parents and wife did not survive the camps), but instead he seeks and finds meaning in his life experiences. Unlike Freud, his analysis looks to the future rather than the past, and unlike some of the existentialists, he focuses not on life's absurdity or meaninglessness, but on its possibilities and its responsibilities. Life's meaning must transcend both the present moment and the desire of us all to be happy. Happiness is an incidental byproduct of a meaningful life and a meaningful life does not demand instantaneous gratification.

What is so profound about Frankl's thought is that it springs from the nadir of human depravity. He experienced the worst of human behavior and emerged with a manifesto for optimism.

Among all of his descriptions of the unspeakable horrors of the concentration camps, Frankl spends little time dissecting the nature of evil. There is no question, however, that evil exists on a continuum from the intentional social snub to the systematic slaughter of fellow humans.

James Madison in Federalist 10 (remember way back somewhere in your early education you learned that the Federalist papers were written by Hamilton, Madison and Jay to make the case for ratification of our Constitution) describes his fellow citizens as "factious." If there isn't a dispute, they will create one, and the majority will tromp all over the minority if they can. Thus, argues Madison, we need a representative form of government where one person has to speak for the views of many and that mechanism will preserve the rights of the minority while, at the same time, knocking the rough edges off the will of the majority.

There is evidence, and I am not at this late date going to insert a footnote so you'll just have to trust me, that the excesses of cruel behavior are exacerbated by a group. Whether it is the ratification of others being there, or the sense of belonging, or a sense of safety from repercussions, the group magnifies the human tendency toward cruelty.

Here comes the inevitable segue back to rowing. Suffering, meaningfulness and groups—rowing has them all. We practice not just to get better at rowing, but to learn to endure discomfort. Pain. Disappointment. Failure. All of them teach us lessons that are absolutely transferrable to everything else we do in life.

Meaningfulness or goals is Frankl's major point and is the stock and trade of every coach, every motivational speaker, every decent teacher. Experience is one of the three ways Frankl says we can find meaning, but what kind of experience? Fortunately, you are not the first person in the history of the world to ask that question. Virtually every philosopher mentioned in this book gives some guidance on what kind of experience is useful in squeezing the last drop of meaning out of our short time on this earth. So should you read philosophy? Have you been paying attention?

Thinkers from the beginning of human history have recognized human evil, cruelty and selfishness. The Garden of Eden metaphor in the book of Genesis is an example. Adam and Eve are in paradise—until they screw it up and get kicked out. We continue to live in an abundant earth, until we pollute the oceans, the air, the soil. We live in a state of perpetual warfare and have the nuclear capability of total self-destruction. We know better, yet we are simply powerless to check our baser impulses. Therein, in my opinion, is the root of religion: we need a supernatural force to save us from ourselves.

Religion requires belief, and for this book, I am more interested in reason. While I have many a quarrel with organized religion, I do not discount the value of religion to those who take support or comfort from it, or who use it as a vehicle to express awe, wonder or thankfulness.

We may not be able to control the actions of others, but, by the same token, we can choose not to let the actions of others control us. Of my two neighbors, one was cheery and each morning greeted the other with good wishes for the day. The response was a non-response: a scowl or at best a grunt. I asked the cheery one, "why do you continue to engage him?" The response was, "why should I let him dictate my behavior?" Cruelty doesn't have to beget cruelty, and indeed, that is the message of the Christian gospels. It is just easier to say than to do.

CHAPTER 35

Time

> "What then is time? If no one asks me, I know what it is. If I wish to explain it to him who asks, I do not know." St. Augustine

Imagine, if you can, a modern society without time. It could be utopian, where everything happens when it should: where meals appear when hunger dictates, where the cycles of day and night, the sun and the moon, the tides and the seasons allow or compel behavior and where meetings of humans are entirely random. But for most of us, timelessness would be chaos. How can you catch a plane when there is no schedule? Can a factory run when the workers show up whenever they feel like it? Is it reasonable or even possible to plan anything without a schedule? We are absolutely time-bound because time is the organizing principle of civilization in at least six ways.

Sequence is the first. We, and most philosophers, view time as linear, so b happens after a and c cannot happen without both a and b. If time were nebular so that things just spin around and the sun may come up in the middle of the night or a train may leave the station before the tracks are built, we would be totally confused and disoriented. Things happen in patterns and we have learned to prepare each step to enable the next, or at least that is the way we have come to expect that things will work.

Duration is the second organizing principle. If a church sermon goes more than 15 minutes, we start to squirm (if it is a bad one, five minutes is enough). The work day traditionally is eight hours, we sleep for eight and expect the phone to be answered in four rings. We allow for some cultural variations. For example a dinner of friends in France may last for three hours while dinner in an American family may be fifteen minutes if it happens at all. But if guests drop in unexpectedly and are still there three days later, we perceive that something is seriously out of whack. The same might not be true in India.

Planning is next. We pay our taxes by April 15th. We can count on it so the IRS can't and doesn't come knocking on the door for next year's taxes in December. We know the tide will come in twice a day, so if we are going to get the boat we grounded afloat again, that is when to do it. If we want to hold a meeting, we give a time and location so people can show up. We don't pay much attention to the natural cycles of the moon waxing and waning or the seasons progressing, but with climate change giving us unaccustomed heat and cold waves, mother nature is fighting back and saying "you are screwing up, humans." Deadlines are a critical part of planning and as a lawyer if you want to get sued, just let the statute of limitations expire and your former client will be asking you to pay his claim. Time is not just an organizing principle; it has consequences.

Rhythmic recurrence should probably head the list because it is based on the natural phenomena of seasons, gestation periods, crop maturities, animal migrations and the like. Farmers don't need a clock to know when the soil is warm enough to plant, but knowing when the sheep were impregnated or when the tomatoes will be ripe helps to plan. In a post-industrial society, the school year, work week and national holidays are templates with which we organize our lives.

Synchronizing actions means we do things that require coordination according to the clock. If the game starts at 1 p.m., the fans and television all are ready then, and they would be annoyed more than somewhat if they arrived only to learn that the players had decided to play at 9 a.m. and the game was over. A parade wouldn't be much of a parade if the drums all beat at random, the marchers wandered around aimlessly and the crowd blocked the street.

Finally, **time perspective**, or how we view time, controls our lives. We are young or old, both chronologically and in how we view ourselves. We are more interested in the future than the past or vice versa. We either think we have too much time and are bored, or we are frantic to accomplish more than time allows. In all cases, time is the measure even though time is an artificial construct of our civilization like money or corporations or, dare I say it, religions.

So why write about time in a book on rowing and philosophy? The rowing part is easy. You can't (and I defy you to try) row in a multi-person boat without sequence: if the leg drive happens before the hands are away you may flip over backwards; if the stroke rate is thirty-two and you are rowing sixteen you will get slammed in the back with an oar handle; if you don't plan to get to practice on time you will watch from the shore; if you have no rhythm and can't synchronize your stroke, your rowing sucks; and if you aren't focused on the next race then the last one better have been good, because that is all you have going for you.

Philosophy and philosophers are consumed with time because they want to understand and explain it. Heraclitus, the fifth-century-BCE sophist, in telling us that we cannot step into the same river twice, is using a metaphor to say that time will have made the molecules of water different because the world is in flux and there are no absolutes. (Plato will later attempt to destroy this position, thus launching the ever present debate between the relativists and the absolutists.)

Aristotle tells us that our experience of time is only of the momentary present. He writes: "Whether if mind did not exist, time would exist or not, is a question that may be fairly asked; for if there cannot be someone to count there cannot be anything that can be counted." So if the tree falls in the woods and no one is there to hear it, does it make a sound? We know, by now, that philosophers like to ask questions to which they are not prepared to give a clear answer.

St. Augustine enters into the fray by saying that time itself is not real, but exists only in the "mind's counting," whereas St. Thomas Aquinas portrays God as the master watchmaker who keeps the universe functioning. Kant says that our mind structures our experience like a mathematical line and time is, therefore, a form of consciousness with its own reality. William James sees time as a "specious present" with a broad reach before and after the present that influences our psychological understanding of what is happening—in other words, our consciousness.

Time is, of course, what history is about—placing non-simultaneous events in a linear sequence and trying to make sense of what has happened to help us understand the present and prepare for the future. Then there is Einstein's theory of relativity where potentially time can become a circular loop. If you now think I am going to try to explain Einstein, you are very, very wrong. I will go with Woody Allen who says that time is nature's way of keeping everything from happening at once.

The brilliant German writer Thomas Mann valued the transitoriness of life. Without a beginning and an end, birth and death, there is no meaning. Timelessness, where there never was anything new and the old never passed away, would be stagnant and totally uninteresting—uninspired. Time, therefore, is a gift. And surely, to the rower, to be stagnant, in water or ability, is to be full of noxious vapors. There is no health in it.

One of my rowing friends made an interesting connection between rowing and the often stated desire of adults to go back to the womb. Rowing has rocking like in the cradle. Our bodies go back and forth on every stroke. What's more, we are wearing spandex that is like swaddling clothes and we take water bottles in the boat to suck on. Yikes.

CHAPTER 36

Jefferson, James, Dewey, and Rorty

"Men are the freest when they are most unconscious of freedom."
D. H. Lawrence

I was standing there with a bottle of goat's milk in each hand and some empties under my arm when he came across the street, pot-belly leading the way, scowl and menace right behind. Was I going to steal his mail—on a Sunday morning no less? He had lived there for forty years and trouble had never found him but he was willing to shoot me if I interloped. The sign in his yard in big bold hand-made letters urged a vote against all incumbents, all of whom, along with government itself, are corrupt scum-suckers.

I introduced myself, suggested that shooting me would be in bad taste, and told him that we were caring for his neighbor's goats while they were out of town. He still didn't like me scoping out his territory but conceded that I had "business" in the neighborhood, and notwithstanding my disreputable appearance, I was not likely to abuse his mail box.

I actually kind of liked this guy (unlike Mr. Shirtless with the baseball bat who deduced that a dog was a dog—him I would be glad not to see again). Here's the question though: what about those who are angry, suspicious, hostile and dogmatic? Is this a problem that philosophy can address? Should I have laid a few Aristotelian licks on him with a dash of Nietzsche for good measure? He might have stood still for Thomas Jefferson, but what would he have made of the American pragmatists: William James, John Dewey and Richard Rorty?

Jefferson wrote that he had sworn eternal hostility toward all forms of tyranny over the mind of man. This guy (the mailbox owner) saw tyranny everywhere, but he still believed in the vote—in self-determination. Granted his yard sign didn't set out his complete political philosophy, but he clearly signed on to Jefferson's life (safety), liberty, and the pursuit of happiness. And being left the hell alone. Jefferson said that too: that the government that governs best governs least. Or maybe John Adams, or Thomas Paine or Napoleon or Alfred E. Neuman, said it. Probably they all did.

131

What was so great about his sign, though, is that while all incumbents are crooks, we should VOTE to get them out, and presumably get a new set of crooks in. That is American optimism at its best, and it absolutely fits with Jefferson's view that philosophy is for action.

A democratic government is based on an idea—freedom—so it is, in and of itself, a philosophy. Three great exponents of the philosophy of democracy are William James, John Dewey, and Richard Rorty.

WILLIAM JAMES

James was a medical doctor, psychologist, and philosopher (d. 1910), who held a pragmatic view of the truth. If it works, it is true; if it doesn't, it's false. What is true today may not continue to be true because there are no fixed pole stars and no absolutes. Beliefs can't just sit on their butts in the library; they have to earn their keep by proving themselves in action. In that respect, James is like your rowing coach because you may talk a good game, but what you do with the oar on the water is what counts.

Utility, workability, and satisfactory consequences are the test of an idea. To say what works is true and what is true works are exactly the same thing. He asks: "[W]hat concrete difference will an idea being true make in anyone's life? What is its cash value?" A true thought is an instrument of action, and as such is also an instrument of self-government. But thinking has to be more than simply rearranging our prejudices.

Truth, he says, lives on the credit system. It must continually prove itself or lose its value. Truth is just a collective name for the verification process whereby we test ideas on a day to day basis for their actual use in living our lives. And here is an interesting thought: the greatest enemy of our presently held truths is all of our other truths. Jurist Oliver Wendell Holmes, Jr. put it this way: "...the best test of truth...is to get itself accepted in the competition of the market." Truth, however, is fragile and truth misunderstood becomes a dangerous lie.

The marketplace of ideas is the primary justification for freedom of speech as it is protected by the First Amendment of the Constitution. Good ideas will rise to the top and bad ones will sink of their own weight. (In case you are interested, other justifications for free speech are venting—talk non-sense, but don't hose me down with an Uzi; self-fulfillment, and using speech as a tool of change in a democratic government.) It is a pretty tidy package of how a democracy works, actually, particularly when tied to James's concept of free will.

Experience has a way of "boiling over" and making us change our present formula of what is true and verifiable. Our first act of freedom, if we are free, is to affirm that we are free. That means we take action on the best information we have today, and if it turns out tomorrow to be wrong, we don't cloak ourselves in regret, but simply correct our course with the new truth we have found. This is neither infatuated optimism nor heartless self-interest, but rather a collective hope based on a continuing, energetic and optimistic search for the truth. So, he said, we have to live today by what truth we can get but be prepared tomorrow, on better evidence, to call it falsehood.

ROWTON

Ha, you thought I was asleep. So, if one subscribes to this kind of pragmatism, it would be hard to be an ideologue because the truth is too transitory. Well, I suppose you could be a zealot for one idea today and the opposite tomorrow. Describes current politics pretty well.

As a pragmatist, James was distrustful of dogma, but he did make an argument for certainty with his analogy of the mountain climber who has reached a crevasse he must jump (he can't go around or back). Isn't it better that he be certain he can make the leap successfully than to launch himself into space thinking there is no way he can make it? Coaches call this "visualization," Norman Vincent Peale called it "the power of positive thinking," others call it confidence or stupidity or ignorance, but I will go with Henry Ford who said that those who think they can and those who think they can't are both right.

JOHN DEWEY

Known best as an educator, Dewey (d. 1952) was a champion of experience as the ultimate teacher. Not just any old experience, mind you, but experience that looked back and forward and served as a platform for further learning. He saw knowledge as transitory, and the purpose of life as keeping the mind free. Brilliant, maybe, but he had a writing style described as having the monotonous consistency of peanut butter.

Democracy is the best form of government because it requires the engagement of its citizens and utilizes their individual talents. He makes one of the clearest arguments for equal opportunity by acknowledging that people have unequal talents, and without free opportunity, the more talented could oppress the less gifted. (There is a Russian proverb just to the opposite: "we must help the talented; the untalented will make it on their own.") For Dewey, the democratic faith in equality is that each individual should have the chance to contribute what he or she can and it is the sum total of those contributions that matters.

As to the elitist disdain for the common person, he acknowledged that the unwashed may not be very wise: "But there is one thing they are wiser about than anybody else can be, and that is where the shoe pinches, the troubles they suffer from." The goal is for every citizen to have freedom of mind. He had faith in human intelligence and in government that allowed and compelled participation. He also distrusted wealth. Dewey agreed with Louis Brandeis that "we can have a democratic society or we can have a concentration of great wealth in the hands of a few, but we cannot have both."

While Dewey thought democracy was an expedient for allowing individual growth, the test was whether those governed had a share in their management. If not, then Dewey was with Jefferson who wrote in the Declaration of Independence that when the government fails to protect life, liberty, and the pursuit of happiness, it is the right and duty of the people to change it and institute in its place, a government that does. Jefferson recognized that change can be dangerous: "Anyone who has begun to think places some portion of the world in jeopardy."

That is radical thought, by the way. Those in power will never acknowledge that they are oppressors, and those with great wealth will always have opportunities completely out of the grasp of the poor, particularly when, as now, the Supreme Court of the United States has basically said money is speech and the more money you have, the more speech you get. Jefferson would weep.

But enough depressing drivel; bring on Dewey the rower. We learn, he says, by what we do. Life is about the present and the future, not the past. We can look backward to learn from the issues of the past, but education is comprised of sequential experiences, each one building on those that have come before. All education is based on habit. Every experience modifies the person and the quality of the next experience and the one after that. Habit is an attitude. It is a way of making things happen. One could substitute the word PRACTICE for habit, and John Dewey would be your rowing coach.

Here is what Dewey had to say about intensive learning and physical activity: "[P]eriods of genuine reflection only [occur] when they follow after times of more overt action and are used to organize what has been gained [when] the hands and other parts of the body besides the brain are used." You may think that when you have rowed to exhaustion, your mind is fried, but in fact Dewey thought that we learn all sorts of things in addition to what we think we are studying, and the mind is churning away after we have used our bodies. If true, this is a pretty good argument why athletics should be a part of education.

Education is a social process. It takes place though the interaction of people. Consensus (as in democracy) requires communication but that communication is meaningful only insofar as it leads to action. Part of what we learn is informal through the ordinary companionship of adults and youth, and part is directed and intentional through our formal education.

Philosophy, Dewey said, is thinking which has become conscious of itself—thinking caused by the unsettled nature of human existence—thinking about what choices we have and how we might put them into—you got it—action! Here we need a big drum roll because if education is the forming of fundamental dispositions, intellectual and emotional, toward nature and our fellow man, then philosophy can be defined as the general theory of education. Philosophy is education. Ta ta.

Since it has shrugged on the garment of education, philosophy can't just lounge around. It has two fundamental tasks, both of which have to do with hard science—facts that are verifiable. The first is to be a critic of how science is currently being used, pointing out what values are "obsolete" or "sentimental"; and second, directing how new discoveries in science can be useful to our society.

If there were such as office as American Philosopher in Chief, John Dewey would hold it.

RICHARD RORTY

I include Richard Rorty (d. 2007), one of today's thought leaders, because he so aptly describes what the philosophy of hope of John Dewey, William James, and poet Walt Whitman has meant to American democracy, and how that philosophy—that "can do-ism"—has been scorched by the unfortunate wars of the second half of the twentieth and the first decade of the twenty-first centuries. The cultural retreat toward cynicism and self-interest, away from reason and back to religion has left us in a national malaise. Rorty suggests a tonic that will reinvigorate us.

National pride is to countries, he says, as self-respect is to individuals: a necessary condition for self-improvement. It is a delicate balance between too much goose-stepping, lebensraum type national pride and so little that moral courage and civic engagement are not possible. To love one's country leads to both pride and shame, and for a real debate about our national direction to occur, the pride has to outweigh the shame. Ordinary citizens have to feel empowered enough to care.

It is the poets, the writers, and the singers who tell a nation's story. What a nation has been and what it strives to be depends on what events the poet or singer chooses to glorify or demean, and the result, if it is effective, seldom reflects the truth, the whole truth and nothing but the truth. What it does reflect is our moral identity—how we see ourselves and how we judge our collective selves.

What Dewey, Whitman, and others were doing was to cast America as a society that has cut itself free from the fear of religion and has tied its wagon to the polestar of caring for one another. They wanted Americans to take pride in each other. They saw hope as replacing fear in a thoroughly secular society. They saw social justice as the driving force behind the philosophy of Americanism. The human adventure, for them, was one that only looked forward toward utopia. "The United States themselves are essentially the greatest poem" wrote Whitman.

This was the philosophy of the Roosevelts—Teddy and Franklin D.—one a Republican and the other a Democrat. But according to Rorty, the second half of the twentieth century and the first decade of the twenty first have left this optimism in the ditch.

Rorty's solution is to forget about truth as the object of inquiry and to seek, instead, consensus about the ends to be achieved and then to work on the details for getting there. This is pragmatism to its core. The "*isms*" and the labels get in the way of doing what needs to be done, and for this obstruction*ism*, philosophy is hardly blameless.

Rorty's point is that intellectuals have been too quick to jettison national pride. There is lots to criticize and to be ashamed of in our national dittybag, but loving someone, or something, like our country, gives us those contrary impulses of wishing the best on the one hand and being super critical on the other. If America's trump card is hope, then we have to rediscover the American optimists. That would mean changing from Politics (where the party and its insatiable appetite for power is supreme) to politics (where solutions for the common good are sought) because, according to English historian, Lord Acton, "liberty is not a means to a higher political end, it is itself the highest political end."

CHAPTER 37

Rowology Redux

> "You cannot step into the same river twice; for fresh waters are ever flowing in upon you." Heraclitus of Ephesus (d. 480 BCE)

We have visited a lot of philosophers and a lot of rowing strokes. As we go through life we pick up little gems of information that combine to make up who we are and what we believe. Since we are constantly in a state of flux, beliefs change, but the process of wondering and thinking and deciding what we believe is constant. Another constant is that you probably will not go back to the first chapter and revisit Rowology even if I suggest you should, so, here it is again as a wrap up of this clam bake. Perhaps this will prove what Heraclitus said, that we cannot step into the same river twice.

NUMBER ONE

Efficiency. You can't win a race if you are not efficient. Fly and die. That is the fate of crews that go out too fast and can't sustain the pace. Life, rowing and philosophy all share the virtue of efficiency. Not wasting time, energy, emotion, and happiness is a virtue.

Efficiency is getting maximum power out of each stroke; maximum benefit out of each thought; maximum enjoyment out of each day. We live in a universe of limited resources, even if we who are blessed to live in the U.S. of A. don't acknowledge it. If we don't use our talents, our resources, our opportunities efficiently, then we squander them and when they are gone they are GONE.

NUMBER TWO

Steadfastness. This is an old-fashioned, even biblical sounding word. What it means at its root is hanging in there. You can't quit 750 meters into a race. You owe it to your fellow crewmembers to die first. Woody Allen said that 95 percent of life is showing up, but that other 5 percent is a bitch. It means you can't quit.

It means you finish what you started. It means no matter how terrible your case gets, how many witnesses go south, how hateful the judge's rulings, you hang in there because you owe it to your client and to yourself.

It means that even if you think every politician is a crook, every decision biased, every new law designed to benefit the least deserving, you do not give up on democracy because it is the only system where hope is built in. You persevere because that is the way you are put together, that is the way you are trained and that is all you know how to do.

NUMBER THREE

Courage. What I mean here is moral courage: doing what you know is right no matter what the personal cost. And there will be a substantial personal cost, believe me. Lost friends. Lost business. Lost opportunities. You have heard the saying: "To get along, go along." That is the moral philosophy of a salamander. Moral courage costs plenty. Going along is free. Here is what Ernest Hemmingway said about it:

"Moral courage is a rarer commodity than bravery in battle or great intelligence. Yet it is the one essential, vital quality of those who seek to change a world which yields most painfully to change." *A Farewell to Arms*

Moral courage is Martin Luther King, Jr. writing to his fellow (white) clergy and saying: "I am in the Birmingham jail because I am black. What are you going to do about it?" The answer, unfortunately, was, not much.

Moral courage is the home school parent, the animal rescue saint, the gardener who wants to reduce her carbon footprint. Moral courage isn't written in capital letters; it is a matter of every day actions that consciously benefit others than ourselves. It is not laughing at a racist joke, redoing a poorly done job, saying "I'm sorry."

Does rowing teach moral courage? No, not explicitly. But it does teach physical courage and the two are connected. Courage is the willingness to sacrifice for someone else. It is the spirit and the power that says: "This has to be done. I will do it." It is the selflessness that recognizes that no one of us is the center of the universe and that there are goals and causes greater than ourselves to be served. That is courage, be it moral or physical, and any life lesson that can teach it is valuable.

NUMBER FOUR

Being an amateur. What an insult. What a putz. Somebody who is a dabbler; a swell who has no talent. As David Halberstam recognized, rowers are the ultimate amateurs because there are no professionals. Bless the sport for that.

The forest would be very silent indeed if only those birds sang that sing best. Amateur means a lover of the activity and you won't find a more romantic group than rowers. They do it because they love it and they work voluntarily (and we're talking real work here—lost skin, sore muscles and an occasional unscheduled throw up). When they are supposed to be doing other work, they fantasize about rowing because it is so compelling. That is an amateur all right: someone who is so consumed with a sport that it becomes a philosophy of life—a metaphor—a Rowology.

Let's see if we can put some component parts together: discipline, strength, compatibility, teamwork, aesthetics, fun, timing, control, power. Can you really harness all of that together and still be an amateur? Absolutely.

NUMBER FIVE

Transcendence. Or maybe you prefer the word spirituality? Both of them turn me on, actually. Transcendence: to catapult out of the earth-bound to some cosmic venue; or spirituality where we cuddle up to the Luminous Unknown and bask in the glory of it all. What I have in mind is a little more mundane, but still it has some of the shimmery, frosted flakiness of that heavenly stuff.

I'm talking about oneness with the water; oneness with my body; oneness with the universe. I'm thinking of motion that is continuous and seamless and fluid. I'm thinking of a mind that is completely focused and, paradoxically, completely at rest.

Either word—spirituality or transcendence—defines itself reluctantly. The concept is illusive, ever deepening and ultimately ephemeral. We sense it, as the Apostle Paul said, "through a glass darkly."

But they—it—the sensation is real and undeniably part of rowing whether in a single on flat water early in the morning when the rest of the city is still damp and groggy, or in an eight that has started magically to swing. And when you have achieved the perfect catch where your oar grips the water and every ounce of your power flows through your body to propel the boat, then you are transported, both physically and spiritually. No kidding. Thing is, though, there is no time to pose and admire it like a golfer following his shot, because you have to do it all over again for the next stroke and the stroke after that and on into eternity.

There is a heightening of the senses here, most notable in a single, where you can feel every part of your body and the harmony of each stroke. You can close your eyes and sense the water, your balance as you come up the slide, your feet as you make small corrections in your course. Remember to open your eyes before you crash into that snag.

NUMBER SIX

Self-knowledge. You can't get it without pain. A trial lawyer mentor of mine said that he never learned anything from a case he won. That doesn't mean you try to lose a few just for the education, but it is true that life's hard lessons are the ones that smack us up-side the head. Those are the lessons that do not have to be repeated. Eleanor Roosevelt urged us to "learn from the mistakes of others. You do not have time to make them all yourself."

That is why I favor racing even if you aren't strong or experienced or don't foolishly crave medals (forget about attention—nobody else cares). Racing teaches us about ourselves; about our limitations and how we arbitrarily set them; about courage and how we seldom test it; about preparation and how we often neglect it. These are the lessons that show how plastic our lives are and how we can stretch and change and grow.

Can rowing make you a better scholar? Mental toughness and mental discipline are not that different from their physical siblings. It is all one body, and self-awareness, and self-evaluation come out of the same head.

NUMBER SEVEN

Celebration. We don't celebrate enough and that is a shame because it is one activity that brings us together and builds community. I'm not just talking about the jumping up and down and hugs and high fives and photos after the race. Celebration is in order on the nastiest day when it is cold and choppy and wet because it is a gift to just be out there doing something you love.

Celebration links up with the spiritual because we are thankful for what we have been given and for our friends, and what we have achieved together. We have created a bond and in that sense we know we are not alone and abandoned in the universe. So put that in your pipe and smoke it you depressing existential fatalists (who actually claim you are optimists).

NUMBER EIGHT

Aesthetics. Why do farmers plant flowers? Because humankind cannot live without beauty. "If you have but two pennies, buy a loaf of bread with one and a lilly with the other." I quote the last because I got it from somewhere—probably a famous philosopher. You no doubt have deduced that the ethical system of Rowology actively encourages filching ideas, thoughts and even whole concepts from others without attribution. While I do not recommend this in school papers, I do think that philosophy and ideas are to be shared. They are in the best sense, open source, because every idea should interact with every other.

Rowing is infused with beauty from the shape and design of the boats to the grace and power of the sport itself. There is beauty in the motion without noise, in the flow of the boat through the water, and in being part of something that is somehow larger than our own lives.

There is beauty in the seasons as the willows along the riverbank quicken in the spring or the leaves color or the mist ebbs and flows as if it were alive. There is beauty in the banks where the salmon spawn and the beavers chew and the ducks hang out. There is beauty in weighing enough (stopping) to let a mother duck with her chicks in a line astern pass by.

So, in sum, does rowing solve the philosophical questions posed from time immemorial? It helps, but like so many questions, the answer depends on what framework, what life view, what baggage we bring. I think grabbing our preconceptions, shaking them by the scruff of the neck and making them earn their keep on the shelves of our minds is healthy—necessary even. The best way I have found to steam clean the brain is to row to exhaustion.

So there it is—again—the big eight principles of Rowology. It is not enough for a world-view, but it is a start. The life of the mind is a thrilling adventure, every bit as engaging as the sports we encounter in the life of the body. Philosophy is our intrepid guide in the journey of the mind, and its waterways are full of surprise, delight, frustration, and peril.

CHAPTER 38

The Long Haul

"What if the hokey pokey really **is** what it's all about?" Bumper Sticker

Constant means going on all the time. Races, on the other hand, are episodes. Car wrecks are episodes. Meals are episodes. As exciting or fulfilling or terrifying as episodes are, most of our lives consist of doing what we do—working, or studying or feeding the kids or cleaning the house. Being constant. So how do we achieve the good life if so much of it is mundane and regular and predictable? The answer has to be to find a way to make the mundane unpredictable or, if that isn't possible, to find the nuance in the predictable.

I am going to preempt any wiseass comments by the Rowton here and lay out the four elements of a strategy for enlivening the mundane and giving it a leading role in promoting our good life. The first is **amplified awareness**.

Suppose mowing the lawn is a regular part of your chores and the damn grass keeps growing and you have to keep cutting it. What a pain. But what if you ditch the headphones and concentrate on the pattern of the mow, and try to make the lines absolutely straight or aesthetically significant? What if, instead of letting the music numb your brain, you let the constancy of the noise that filters through your ear plugs host whatever thoughts filter into your brain? What if you concentrate on relaxing every muscle you are not actively using?

The point of amplified awareness is that if we are doing something that we have to do over and over again, we ought to seek out the nuance, the variation, the shades and colors of it. The more we are "into it," the more we will get out of it, even if mowing the grass doesn't rank up there with golf and skiing in the enjoyment department.

The second strategy is **embracing practice**. Ninety-five, maybe 99 percent of the time you spend on any sport is practice. Practice is the constant so we need to find a way to make practice meaningful. Every superior athlete I have known practiced well. In rowing that means analyzing every stroke, concentrating during every piece, never dogging it and never checking out and never cruising. Mindful repetition leads to the discovery of subtle variations, and the awareness of those variations leads to better practice and eventually that practice will make you a better rower. Indeed, human expertise, says philosopher Hubert Dreyfus, comes from a variety of situations all seen from the same perspective but requiring different tactical decisions. So if you want to be an expert rower, you have to practice and race enough that you develop the ability to respond to any situation.

But when practice becomes license to drift, literally and figuratively, then practice is wasted and my money is on the person in the seat behind you who is concentrating so thoroughly that she isn't even aware that you are goofing off. In practice, time is the teacher, patience is the mentor, and perfection is the cloud-obscured peak that we will never quite reach. But if practice becomes a search for the "feel," the effortless effort, the perfect catch, then practice becomes compelling, and exciting and even fun.

Third we need **constant assessment**. You probably think: "yeah, I practiced my butt off all season, and my erg scores stayed the same and the coach still doesn't know my name, and I am in the third boat rowing with the shit-birds." Maybe so, but the nature of sport, and of life, is that we are on a plateau most of the time. We have to learn to love the plateau.

When we first start a sport, we improve rapidly for a while, then backslide, and then level off. If we keep at it and practice while we are on the plateau then sooner, but more probably later, we will have another episode of gains, and some fall back and then another slightly higher plateau, and so it goes. We can't really predict when the surges will come, so the challenge is to embrace the plateau and stay on the course we have set—practicing as well as we can, and not getting frustrated or impatient or petulant. After all, boredom is an obsessive search for novelty where no novelty may exist. Constancy is accepting the plateau as our normal and doing everything we can to make the normal exciting and fruitful. Nietzsche says: "[L]ife is a hundred times too short for us to bore ourselves."

Fourth is **dedication**. Mastery of rowing or of any other aspect of life, yes, even mowing the lawn, is recognizing that we are part of a process, and what happens during that process is often more important than what happens at the end. We are constantly in the process of becoming and like love or democracy, there is no goal line. Think of the water as the world, and the boat as your vehicle, and you as the creator (small "c"). How rewarding your journey is, in life or in rowing, will depend on what you create, and dedication is the key to that creation. If I were to identify a single characteristic of homo sapiens (us, but luckily not the Rowton), it is that we are learners. And the real key to a fulfilling life is learning how to learn on the plateau, with the mundane, the long haul, the stretch, the highway through Kansas.

Rowton

I saw this coming a mile away, and I bet you did too. Now he is going to say that it is the journey that counts and not all those medals he craves.

It is the journey that counts and not the medals. Here is the true confession. I love the medals because they mean we won. We achieved something and they are the material manifestation of it. (Plato would say that the medals, if made by an artisan are just a reflection of the real FORM, and if made by an artist are a poor and misleading reflection of a reflection. Aristotle would probably like them just fine.)

I found an antique brass towel rack with three arms and a nice round filial on top and I put it in my study and hung all my medals on it where I could see them every day and, not incidentally, they could be admired by anyone who came to my office (as if they cared). It was my vanity in full flower. Then as we were packing to move, Leah, my wife of over four decades, suggested that there was no place for the medal rack in the new and smaller house. Crap. I pouted for a few days, then packed up the medals in a box with other memorabilia I never look at, and sold the towel rack at the garage sale.

I am not saying my blood lust for medals is gone—just that what I appreciate about rowing is so much more than the medals. It is the constancy of it in my life. It is the physical manifestation of so many other searches and quests and studies and relationships. I feel as if I am on a goalless journey that is far beyond winning because it is a process of refining my stroke that I practice and practice and practice some more. It is the elixir of being alive.

Appendices

Appendix I

> "When the only tool you have is a hammer, every problem begins to resemble a nail." Abraham Maslow

Since philosophy examines how humans deal with ideas, I thought I would pose a few philosophical questions you might want to ponder when sitting in a boat, or perhaps, in the smallest room in your house. Or wherever.

1. Are ideas innate (somehow present in the ether) or must they be perceived from experience?

2. Do morals reside only within a community or are they inherent and independently discoverable?

3. Is sin original, acquired or does it exist at all? ("Don't lead us into temptation. Just point us in the general direction and we will find it ourselves.")

4. Does free will exist?

5. Can lying be justified? I know a woman who says: "I do all the lying for the family. He (her husband) is such a terrible liar."

6. Can we escape the gravitational pull of prejudice, preconception, and ideology?

7. Can intentions without action be courageous?

8. Can morally just actions be cowardly?

9. For courage to be real, must it be accompanied by fear?

10. What is truth? (One of the metaphysical big three.)

11. What is beauty? (One of the metaphysical big three.)

12. What is justice? (One of the metaphysical big three.)

13. What is the opposite of truth? Falsehood, ignorance, pride, hypocrisy, stupidity?

14. Is truth ever frontally naked?

15. Is truth like Dorothy Sayre's cows: If you look at it in the face long enough, it will run away?

16. Is truth like horseshoes, nukes and grenades—close is good enough?

17. Is there a practical application for theoretical knowledge of the metaphysical kind?

18. How do we escape bad choices?

19. How do we get assurance that our beliefs are reasonable?

20. Is happiness simply the result of a bad memory?

21. Nietzsche says: "what does not kill me makes me stronger." If it does kill you, then what?

Happy pondering, and if it is any comfort, remember that the philosophers summarized here are all over the place on these questions, and the answer that works for you today might change tomorrow.

Appendix II

"Nothing so absurd can be said that some philosopher had not said it."
Cicero

A philosopher named William Peppernell Montague devised what he called a metaphysical compass to help us lesser mortals navigate the airy-fairy world of abstract thought. The points of what looks like a baseball diamond are schools of philosophy he chose to acknowledge.

Appendices

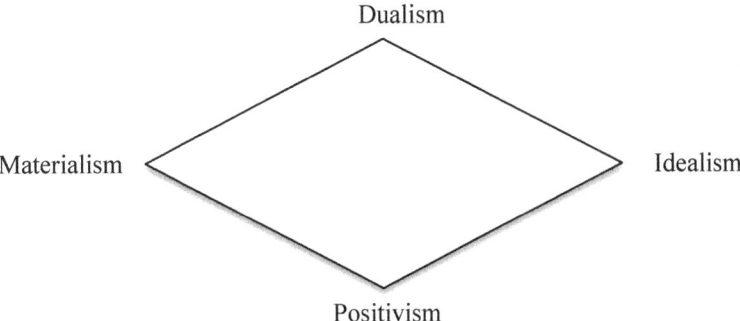

Since philosophers talk to each other and nobody else much cares, W. H. Sheldon took up the model, squished it a bit and came up with this:

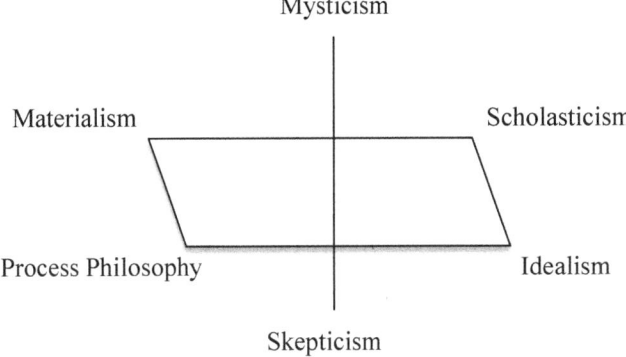

Now here is the absolutely astounding fact that will persuade even my pointy-headed philosopher friends that philosophy and Rowology are inextricably linked. Just take these diagrams, puff on it twice and pat the sides, and *voilà!* You get a diagram of the rowing stroke.

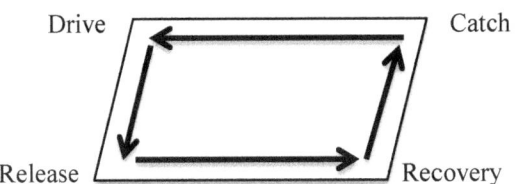

I rest my case.

CPSIA information can be obtained
at www.ICGtesting.com
Printed in the USA
LVOW05*1957290317
527927LV00007BB/29/P

9 781612 299150